STAR WARS

THE CLONE WARS

CHARACTER ENCYCLOPEDIA

THE CLONE WARS are full of heroes and villains, from Anakin Skywalker to General Grievous, as well as characters who would rather not pick a side, such as the pirate Hondo Ohnaka. (As far as Hondo's concerned, he's on his own side!)

In this book, you'll meet more than 200 Jedi, Sith, Senators, clone troopers, fierce creatures, droids, bounty hunters, pirates, and many others. You'll learn new things about who they are, where they come from, and how they are affected by the events of the Clone Wars.

CONTENTS

The characters are arranged in alphabetical order according to their first name, for example Padmé Amidala is under "P." A few characters are listed under their title, such as General Grievous, King Katuunko, and Queen Neeyutnee, but the contents page below lists every character with their page number, so you can find your favorites quickly.

The stories of the Clone Wars continue to be told, so there's a chance you'll meet new characters from adventures that happened a long time ago in a galaxy far, far away...

2-1B DROIDS SERVE AS doctors throughout the galaxy, performing tasks ranging from preventative care to battlefield surgery. They are programmed with medical data about thousands of species, diseases, and treatments.

Voice programmed to sound calm

Servomotor for forearm control

2-1B MEDICAL DROID
GALACTIC MEDIC

STATISTICS

SPECIES: Surgical droid

HEIGHT: 1.5 m (4 ft 11 in)

GENDER: Male programming

ALLIEGIANCE: None

MANUFACTURER: Industrial Automaton

WEAPONS: None

FEATURES: Programmed to treat ailments affecting many species; surgical tools for a variety of situations and uses

Transparent shell over hydraulics

ROBOTIC TLC

2-1B units are in great demand in the Republic fleet, whose capital ships have state-of-the-art medical facilities. After Anakin Skywalker is badly injured above Quell, he is tended to by a medical droid aboard Aayla Secura's Jedi Cruiser.

Magnetized treads for shipboard use

A SPUNKY WED-15 TREADWELL droid, 327-T maintains a number of ship systems aboard the Republic cruiser *Tranquility*, and is assigned to patrol duty after a Separatist agent boards the Jedi Cruiser.

STATISTICS

SPECIES: Repair droid
HEIGHT: 1.24 m (4 ft 1 in)
GENDER: Male programming
ALLEGIANCE: Republic
MANUFACTURER: Cybot Galactica
WEAPONS: None
FEATURES: Telescoping neck; sockets that can be fitted with almost any tool; repair database containing millions of common mechanical items and repair instructions

Binocular, fine-focus vision

Manipulator arm with grasper

327-T
BRAVE MAINTENANCE DROID

Reinforced body brace

GUARD DUTY

327-T is just a maintenance droid, but even a simple treadwell unit can be loyal to the Republic. When told that a Separatist agent is loose aboard the *Tranquility*, 327-T guards the warship's critical reactor room as best his programming will allow.

Rugged treads work in all terrain

4-A7 INTERCEPTS ANAKIN AND Ahsoka on Teth, claiming to be the caretaker of the B'omarr monastery. But he is really a Separatist spy and part of the plot to frame the Jedi for Rotta's kidnapping.

High-band antenna for spy missions

System conduits and powerbus wires

4A-7
SEPARATIST SPY

NO ESCAPE

After sending a holorecording that makes it seem like Anakin and Ahsoka are abusing Rotta, 4A-7's dirty work is done. He heads for the *Twilight* to make his getaway—but is caught by Ahsoka Tano. A saber swing later and 4A-7 is scrap metal.

STATISTICS

SPECIES: Prototype espionage droid
HEIGHT: 1.7 m (5 ft 7 in)
GENDER: Male programming
ALLEGIANCE: Separatists
MANUFACTURER: Arakyd Industries
WEAPONS: None
FEATURES: Programmed for deception; able to speak many languages; concealed holorecorder and transmitter; additional surveillance gear
KNOWN COMPANIONS: Asajj Ventress

Metal feet feature magnetic grip

Vessels of circulatory fluid for surgery

Droid's main logic center

Integrated pallet for surgical use

A4-D
CRUEL CARETAKER

STATISTICS

SPECIES: Supervisor droid
HEIGHT: 1.74 m (5 ft 9 in)
GENDER: Male programming
ALLEGIANCE: Separatists
MANUFACTURER: MerenData
WEAPONS: None
FEATURES: Programmed for surgical procedures; logic center is designed to improve efficiency of procedures and operations
KNOWN COMPANIONS: General Grievous, Gor the Roggwart

FATAL MISTAKE

A4-D monitors the progress of Kit Fisto and Nahdar Vebb, telling his Master of their location and working to improve the odds. He manages to separate Nahdar from his former Master, but loses track of Fisto.

A VETERAN OF MANY BATTLES, Aayla is one of the most skilled Jedi fighters. Instead of the flowing robes worn by traditional Jedi, Aayla favors clothing that won't restrict her movement in combat. Aayla has struggled with emotional attachment and tries to pass on what she has learned.

Lightsaber held in Ataru stance

AAYLA SECURA
ACROBATIC JEDI

STATISTICS

SPECIES: Twi'lek
HEIGHT: 1.78 m (5 ft 10 in)
GENDER: Female
ALLEGIANCE: Jedi Order
HOMEWORLD: Ryloth
WEAPONS: Lightsaber
TALENTS: Remarkable agility; mastery of armed and unarmed combat; meditation on the Living Force
KNOWN COMPANIONS: Anakin Skywalker, Ahsoka Tano, Commander Bly, Kit Fisto

Fitted vest of rycrit hide

Strong, agile legs are weapons too

A MENTOR

The close bond between Ahsoka Tano and Anakin Skywalker reminds Aayla of her own relationship with her former Master Quinlan Vos. When Anakin is badly hurt, Aayla tries to teach Ahsoka to control her emotions: A Jedi can't endanger many lives in trying to save the life of one special person.

A SKILLED NEGOTIATOR, EXPERT pilot, and capable warrior, Adi Gallia sits on the Jedi Council. She is known as one of the Order's wisest diplomats, but can also hold her own in combat.

Saber held ready for Shien mode

FINDING EETH

Some high-ranking Jedi disapprove of Anakin Skywalker, considering him reckless and a poor teacher for Ahsoka Tano. But not Adi. Like him, she is known for her aggressive ways, and has no problem with the Chosen One's quick, decisive action—particularly when Jedi Eeth Koth's life may hang in the balance.

ADI GALLIA
AGGRESSIVE NEGOTIATOR

Armor borrowed from Coruscant Guard

STATISTICS

SPECIES: Tholothian

HEIGHT: 1.84 m (6 ft)

GENDER: Female

ALLEGIANCE: Jedi Order

HOMEWORLD: Coruscant

WEAPONS: Lightsaber

TALENTS: Master of Shien form of lightsaber combat; diplomacy; test piloting the first Jedi starfighters

KNOWN COMPANIONS: Captain Rex, Anakin Skywalker, Yoda, Obi-Wan Kenobi

Flowing tunic allows movement in battle

ANAKIN SKYWALKER'S YOUNG Padawan, Ahsoka, is brave, but also headstrong and reckless. She has much to learn about the ways of the Force—and she must learn them on the battlefield. She soon comes to care for her Master, though he carries secrets that are his alone.

Montrals will grow as Ahsoka matures

Tattoos are part of Togruta culture

Reverse grip is a Shien variant

AHSOKA TANO
PADAWAN AT WAR

STATISTICS

SPECIES: Togruta
HEIGHT: 1.61 m (5 ft 3 in)
GENDER: Female
ALLEGIANCE: Jedi Order
HOMEWORLD: Unknown
WEAPONS: Lightsaber

TALENTS:

Shien style of lightsaber combat; Force sensitivity; exceptional agility

KNOWN COMPANIONS:

Anakin Skywalker, R2-D2, Captain Rex, Plo Koon, Barriss Offee

PADAWAN

Yoda respects Anakin's Force abilities, but worries his emotional attachments will lead him down a dangerous path. By giving him Ahsoka as a Padawan, Yoda hopes Anakin will learn the necessity of letting go. But he comes to wonder if pairing two reckless personalities was wise.

AMIT NOLOFF WAS ONCE A successful spice merchant operating out of Iego. But being trapped in Cliffhold has driven him mad, and he now tells all who will listen about the Curse of Drol, jabbing a finger at Iego's skies by way of wild warning.

Mouth tentacles limp with despair

Rich garments now ruined by poor care

STATISTICS

SPECIES: Quarren
HEIGHT: 1.82 m (6 ft)
GENDER: Male
ALLEGIANCE: Neutral
HOMEWORLD: Iego
WEAPONS: None
TALENTS: Starship piloting; negotiating
KNOWN COMPANIONS: Jaybo Hood

DOOM'S HERALD

Amit Noloff firmly believes that Drol is a vengeful ghost awakened by the Separatists, now seeking revenge against all who try to escape the planet Iego. When Anakin and Obi-Wan get away, he seems almost disappointed.

Stooped posture from frantic pacing

HERALDED AS THE CHOSEN ONE who will bring balance to the Force, Anakin is a young Jedi with astonishing gifts. But he also struggles with his anger, and with secrets he has kept from the Jedi Order. To Yoda, Anakin's destiny remains as clouded as it was when he was a boy.

ANAKIN SKYWALKER
THE CHOSEN ONE

The weapon of a Jedi Knight

Can see things before they happen

Protective armor over Jedi robes

STATISTICS

SPECIES: Human
HEIGHT: 1.85 m
(6 ft 1 in)
GENDER: Male
ALLEGIANCE: Jedi Order
HOMEWORLD: Tatooine
WEAPONS: Lightsaber
TALENTS: Astonishing ability with the Force; expert pilot; knack for fixing machines
KNOWN COMPANIONS: Padmé Amidala, Obi-Wan Kenobi, Ahsoka Tano, R2-D2, Captain Rex

A JEDI'S LIMITS

Even the most powerful Jedi can push himself too far. At Quell, Anakin is badly hurt and is saved thanks only to the efforts of Ahsoka Tano and Aayla Secura. He is anxious to recover, knowing the war will not wait.

Lightweight recon armor

Vehicle control module

STATISTICS

SPECIES: Human
HEIGHT: 1.83 m (6 ft)
GENDER: Male
ALLEGIANCE: Republic
HOMEWORLD: Kamino
WEAPONS: DC-15 blaster pistol
EQUIPMENT: Plastoid armor, surveillance gear

ARF TROOPER
AT-RT RIDER

Powerful limbs can run and jump

SADDLE UP!

ARF troopers consider themselves a breed apart—piloting an AT-RT is more like riding a living thing than driving a vehicle. In fact, many ARF troopers begin their training by riding live mounts.

Toe claws can grapple and cut

13

FARO ARGYUS IS A fifth-generation member of the famed Senate Guard. But he has a secret: He has sold his honor to the Separatists. His first mission is to rescue the Trade Federation's Nute Gunray, who is on his way to Coruscant aboard the Jedi Cruiser *Tranquility*.

Ceremonial crest crowns helmet

ARGYUS
TRAITOR TO THE REPUBLIC

STATISTICS

SPECIES: Human

HEIGHT: 1.83 m (6 ft)

GENDER: Male

ALLEGIANCE: Separatists

HOMEWORLD: Tepasi

WEAPONS: DC-15 blaster pistol

TALENTS: Trained for armed and unarmed combat; knowledge of military tactics and Senate traditions

KNOWN COMPANIONS: Asajj Ventress, Nute Gunray

Blue is traditional Senate Guard color

GUARD DUTY

Nute Gunray's actions on Rodia make him an open enemy of the Republic, and a trial on Coruscant would rally support for the war. Taking care of Gunray is very important to Palpatine, so he entrusts the job to one of his best men: Argyus.

Pale skin bears ritual tattoos

AN ASSASSIN TRAINED IN THE Force by Count Dooku, Ventress burns to be seen as a true Sith, and dreams of the day she will put an end to Obi-Wan Kenobi and Anakin Skywalker. She longs to take their lightsabers as trophies to prove her own worth.

THE MAKING OF A SITH

Those who serve the dark side can expect endless tests—and to be tossed aside as unworthy servants if they fail. Ventress is constantly challenged and responds with animal rage. Such cruel treatment is the way to create new Sith.

Distinctive sun disc of bronzium

Sabers can be joined into deadly saberstaff

STATISTICS

SPECIES: Unknown
HEIGHT: 1.78 m (5 ft 10 in)
GENDER: Female
ALLEGIANCE: Separatists
HOMEWORLD: Unknown
WEAPONS: Lightsabers
TALENTS: Knowledge of the dark side of the Force; fighting with two lightsabers; skilled at infiltration
KNOWN COMPANIONS: Count Dooku, 4A-7, Whorm Loathsom

A CRUEL WOMAN WITH chalk-white skin, Aurra Sing is an infamous pirate and bounty hunter. Rumor has it that she trained as a Padawan, but left the Jedi and is now their sworn enemy. She takes a keen interest in young Boba Fett's upbringing.

Antenna connects to biocomputer

Long, skeletal fingers

AURRA SING
DEADLY HUNTRESS

STATISTICS

SPECIES: Near-human
HEIGHT: 1.83 m (6 ft)
GENDER: Female
ALLEGIANCE: Herself
HOMEWORLD: Nar Shaddaa
WEAPONS: Twin blaster pistols, Czerka Adventurer
TALENTS: Expert sniper; master of hand-to-hand combat; trained spy; biocomputer in head allows surveillance; communications
KNOWN COMPANIONS: Cad Bane, Bossk, Castas, Boba Fett, Hondo Ohnaka

Holsters made of shaak hide

THE HUNTRESS

An expert with her Czerka Adventurer rifle, Aurra is able to hit targets from an incredible distance. Her abilities are an important part of Cad Bane's plan to get past the guards at the Senate building.

Well-worn boots of rancor skin

AN ABLE CLONE PILOT, Axe normally commands the Jedi Cruiser *Resolute*'s Blue Squadron. He flies as Blue Two at the Battle of Ryloth, following the orders of squadron leader Ahsoka Tano.

Unit colors of Blue Squadron

Shoulder bells allow quick maneuvers

Console attaches to chest armor

Elbow guards attach to forearm armor

AXE
BLUE SQUADRON VETERAN

STATISTICS

SPECIES: Human
HEIGHT: 2.08 m (6 ft 10 in)
GENDER: Male
ALLEGIANCE: Republic
HOMEWORLD: Kamino
WEAPONS: DC15 blaster pistol
TALENTS: Expert fighter pilot; trained in military tactics
KNOWN COMPANIONS: Ahsoka Tano, Kickback, Swoop, Tucker

BOSS'S ORDERS

Axe knows that Ahsoka Tano has made a mistake in continuing to press her attack on the Separatist blockade at Ryloth. But when pilots don't obey squadron leaders, the result is chaos. Axe follows orders, but his loyalty ends up costing him his life.

ALDERAAN'S SENATOR, BAIL Organa supports Chancellor Palpatine's efforts to end the Clone Wars and restore peace. He is a friend of Padmé Amidala, the Senator from Naboo, and through her has learned to trust Jedi leaders such as Yoda and Obi-Wan Kenobi.

Robes of wool from Alderaan

BAIL ORGANA
GUARDIAN OF THE REPUBLIC

STATISTICS

SPECIES: Human

HEIGHT: 1.67 m (5 ft 6 in)

GENDER: Male

ALLEGIANCE: Republic

HOMEWORLD: Alderaan

WEAPONS: None

TALENTS: Diplomacy; public speaking; expert knowledge of Republic laws and traditions

KNOWN COMPANIONS: Padmé Amidala, Mon Mothma, Chancellor Palpatine, Yoda, Obi-Wan Kenobi

Practical, well-worn boots of nerf leather

PADMÉ'S SECRETS

Senators need to have a keen eye for people, and Bail Organa guesses that Padmé Amidala and Anakin Skywalker are more than just friends. But Senators also need to be diplomatic, and so Bail never asks Padmé about their relationship.

BARRISS OFFEE HAS BEEN trained in the ways of the Force by the strict Luminara Unduli, and is a loyal, studious Padawan. On Geonosis, she forms an odd friendship with Ahsoka Tano, whose brash ways couldn't be more different.

Tattoos of Mirial initiate

Saber in same style as Master's

SACRIFICE

Deep inside the catacombs on Geonosis, Barriss and Ahsoka find themselves with no way to destroy the Separatists' droid foundry—unless they sacrifice their own lives. They quickly reach the same decision: They will do their duty to ensure a Jedi victory. Fortunately, help arrives just in time.

Rich robes are Mirialan tradition

BARRISS OFFEE
BY-THE-BOOK PADAWAN

STATISTICS

SPECIES: Mirialan
HEIGHT: 1.66 m (5 ft 5 in)
GENDER: Female
ALLEGIANCE: Jedi Order
HOMEWORLD: Mirial
WEAPONS: Lightsaber
TALENTS: Lightsaber combat; Force sensitivity
KNOWN COMPANIONS: Ahsoka Tano, Luminara Unduli

BATTLE DROID
SEPARATIST SOLDIER

B1 BATTLE DROIDS ARE THE soldiers of the Separatists—simple, sturdy machines built by the billions in secret factories and dispatched to attack planets loyal to the Galactic Republic. Clone troopers dismiss battle droids as "clankers," but many have died under their guns.

Antenna receives commands

Simple, cheap vocoder

ROGER ROGER

Some older battle droids have been pushed to their programming limits as the Separatists assign them new duties. Some B1s react by talking endlessly about what they're doing, attempting to handle data overflows in their strained logic modules.

Hand-held scanner for inspections

STATISTICS

SPECIES: Battle droid
HEIGHT: 1.91 m (6 ft 3 in)
GENDER: Male programming
ALLEGIANCE: Separatists
MANUFACTURER: Baktoid
WEAPONS: E-5 blaster rifle
EQUIPMENT: Some units have tougher armor, augmented programming, and other nonstandard features

RECOGNIZABLE BY A YELLOW SPOT on their heads and chests, these droids command squads of regular battle droids, often using military strategies downloaded into their brains. But they're no smarter than rank-and-file droids, to the disgust of Separatist leaders.

Yellow markings indicate rank

Sturdy, no-frills E-5 blaster

Barrel-chested metal chassis

Legs can fold for transport

STATISTICS

SPECIES: Battle droid
HEIGHT: 1.91 m (6 ft 3 in)
GENDER: Male programming
ALLEGIANCE: Separatists
MANUFACTURER: Baktoid
WEAPONS: E-5 blaster rifle
EQUIPMENT: Some units have tougher armor, augmented programming, and other nonstandard features

AWAITING HELP

Battle droid commanders enjoy reminding lesser B1s of their superior rank, but when Jedi or clones are on the loose, they actually hope a tactical droid or other leader will take charge.

NICKNAMED "BETTY DROIDS," these graceful, gleaming mechanicals come in a number of bright colors. They serve wealthy owners as secretaries, butlers, and attendants on worlds such as Coruscant.

Photoreceptors within wide eyes

BD-3000 LUXURY DROID
MAID OF METAL

STATISTICS

SPECIES: Servant droid
HEIGHT: 1.76 m (5 ft 9 in)
GENDER: Female programming
ALLEGIANCE: None
MANUFACTURER: LeisureMech Enterprises
WEAPONS: Usually none
FEATURES: Fluent in around one million languages; can be easily programmed to perform a number of routine tasks; can be programmed for bodyguard duty

Panel hides power recharge socket

Special gyros aid balance sensors

DAMSEL DISTRESS

Most Betty Droids are programmed to act like pretty, slightly dim girls in situations that fall outside of their main functions. This annoys Republic citizens who note that the galaxy is full of smart, strong females such as Padmé Amidala and Luminara Unduli.

TWI'LEK WARRIORS HAVE LONG ridden blurrgs into battle, controlling these fierce steeds with nudges of knees and flicks of reins. They can run as quickly as an AT-RT, and Mace Windu and Cham Syndulla rely on them in their attempt to retake Lessu from the Separatists.

STATISTICS

SPECIES: Blurrg
HEIGHT: 2 m (6 ft 7 in)
HOMEWORLD: Endor & Ryloth
WEAPONS: Fierce bite
ECOLOGY: Endor's blurrgs are placid, slow-moving beasts, but the Rylothian variety has been bred for speed and ferocity

Saddle requires careful balance

Whip-like tail used for defense

Long legs offer surprising speed

Blurrgs eat both plants and meat

BLURRG
BATTLE BEAST

BACK TO BASICS

ARF troopers such as Razor and Stak often begin their training as AT-RT pilots by learning to ride living mounts. On Ryloth, one of Lightning Squadron's AT-RTs breaks down and can't be fixed in time for the assault on Lessu. Cham Syndulla's Twi'leks lend the unlucky trooper a spare blurrg, challenging him to demonstrate his skills in the saddle.

CLONE TROOPER CC-5052, known as Commander Bly, serves with the 327th Star Corps, led by Aayla Secura. He has formed a bond with his Jedi general, and numerous battles have given the 327th a reputation for courage while under Separatist fire.

Bly is an expert shot with DC-17 pistols

Macrobinoculars flip up and down

BLY
ASSISTING AAYLA

Tough, flexible kama indicates high rank

STATISTICS

SPECIES: Human

HEIGHT: 1.83 m (6 ft)

GENDER: Male

ALLEGIANCE: Republic

HOMEWORLD: Kamino

WEAPONS: DC-17 pistols, DC-15 blaster pistol

TALENTS: Armed and unarmed combat; jetpack expertise; knowledge of military tactics; leadership

KNOWN COMPANIONS: Aayla Secura, Captain Rex

LOYAL SOLDIER

Commander Bly has come to admire his Jedi general, respecting Aayla Secura's toughness in a fight and her understanding that personal feelings aren't as important as success on the battlefield. He wishes other Jedi were as focused on their missions.

MEMBERS OF THE 212ᵀᴴ Attack Battalion, Boil and his squadmate Waxer search the outskirts of Nabat for enemy units. When Waxer finds a lost Twi'lek girl, Boil wants no part of looking after her: He's a soldier, not a babysitter. But Numa teaches him the value of humanity in war.

Waxer enjoys mocking Boil's fancy mustache

Comlink antenna built into crest

STATISTICS

SPECIES: Human

HEIGHT: 1.83 m (6 ft)

GENDER: Male

ALLEGIANCE: Republic

HOMEWORLD: Kamino

WEAPONS: DC-15 blaster pistol

TALENTS: Trained for combat, recon, and military tactics

KNOWN COMPANIONS: Waxer, Numa, Commander Cody

BOIL
NABAT'S DEFENDER

FUN MISSIONS

Danger is never far away for clone troopers assigned to scout missions: They will always find themselves out ahead of the main army and under Separatist fire. On Geonosis, Boil and Waxer are sent to find Obi-Wan Kenobi's downed gunship. Getting to the crash site will be hard; getting back alive will be harder.

THE KEEPER OF THE KYBER Crystal, Bolla Ropal and his Padawan, Tyzen Xebec, are sent to Devaron during the Clone Wars. When the bounty hunter Cad Bane catches up with him, brave Ropal refuses to unlock the Kyber Crystal, even though he knows it will cost him his life.

BOLLA ROPAL
MARTYR TO THE FORCE

Green skin reflects reptilian heritage

TERRIBLE PRICE

The Kyber Crystal's list of Force-sensitive children in the galaxy is one of the Jedi Order's secrets, and not the kind of thing a simple hired gun like Cad Bane would know about. Bane's knowledge of it makes Bolla Ropal realize Bane is working for someone who poses a terrible danger to the Jedi Order and could threaten its very future.

Hands have held many Holocrons

Jedi robes command respect on Rodia

STATISTICS

SPECIES: Rodian
HEIGHT: 1.75 m (5 ft 9 in)
GENDER: Male
ALLEGIANCE: Jedi Order
HOMEWORLD: Rodia
WEAPONS: Lightsaber
TALENTS: Force-sensitivity; knowledge of Jedi history

A MEMBER OF COMMANDER WOLFFE'S famed Wolfpack, Boost serves aboard the Jedi Cruiser *Triumphant* and finds himself hunted by Grievous's troops after evacuating the doomed ship. Will the famed Wolfpack meet its end trapped amid the wreckage of a space battle?

Double stripes honor fallen clones

STATISTICS

SPECIES: Human

HEIGHT: 1.83 m (6 ft)

GENDER: Male

ALLEGIANCE: Republic

HOMEWORLD: Kamino

WEAPONS: DC-15 blaster pistol

TALENTS: Combat

KNOWN COMPANIONS:

Sinker, Wolffe, Plo Koon

BOOST
ABREGADO REFUGEE

Helmet bears symbol of the Wolfpack

DC-15 isn't much good in deep space

DON'T GIVE UP

Boost knows he and his comrades are in a tight spot—even a Jedi can't send a signal across the galaxy or defeat all the droids searching for survivors in the Abregado debris. But Boost refuses to give up, convinced somehow rescue will come.

High-traction boot soles

A REPTILIAN BOUNTY HUNTER, Bossk falls in with Aurra Sing's crew of hunters during young Boba Fett's mission to kill the Jedi Master Mace Windu above the planet Vanqor. The chaos of war always brings rich rewards to bold hunters.

Eyes can see in infrared range

BOSSK
TRANDOSHAN THUG

STATISTICS

SPECIES: Trandoshan
HEIGHT: 1.9 m (6 ft 3 in)
GENDER: Male
ALLEGIANCE: Neutral
HOMEWORLD: Trandosha
WEAPONS: Customized blaster rifle, grenade launcher, flamethrower
TALENTS: Starship piloting; blaster fire
KNOWN COMPANIONS: Aurra Sing, Castas, Boba Fett

Bandolier holds pilots' flares

Tough, clawed feet can slash at foes

LIZARD LEGACY

Trandoshans share a star system with the Wookiees, and often raid the Wookiee homeworld of Kashyyyk for slaves. They are fierce warriors and can regrow severed limbs thanks to their reptilian heritage. But this regeneration is slow and painful: Bossk would very much prefer to keep his arms and legs firmly attached to his scaly body.

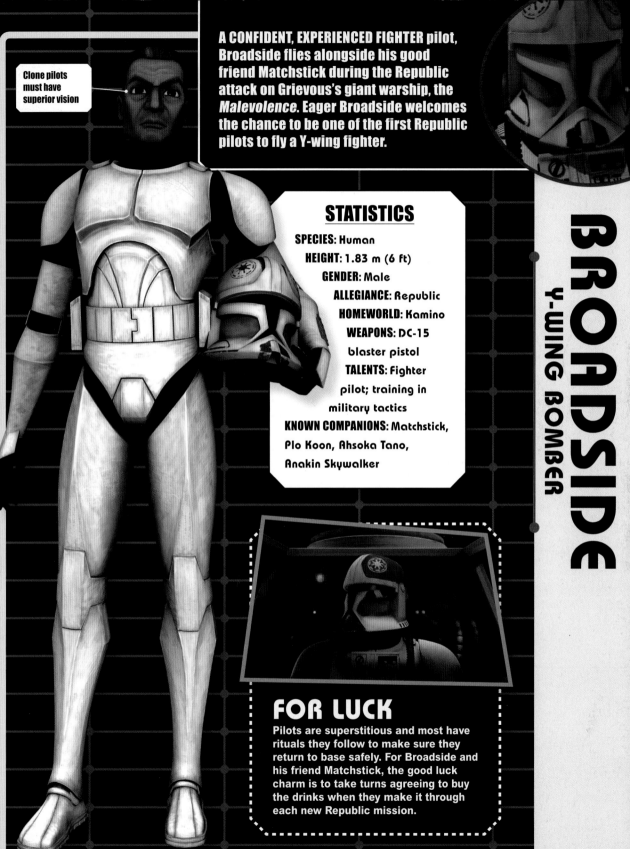

Clone pilots must have superior vision

A CONFIDENT, EXPERIENCED FIGHTER pilot, Broadside flies alongside his good friend Matchstick during the Republic attack on Grievous's giant warship, the *Malevolence*. Eager Broadside welcomes the chance to be one of the first Republic pilots to fly a Y-wing fighter.

STATISTICS

SPECIES: Human
HEIGHT: 1.83 m (6 ft)
GENDER: Male
ALLEGIANCE: Republic
HOMEWORLD: Kamino
WEAPONS: DC-15 blaster pistol
TALENTS: Fighter pilot; training in military tactics
KNOWN COMPANIONS: Matchstick, Plo Koon, Ahsoka Tano, Anakin Skywalker

BROADSIDE
Y-WING BOMBER

FOR LUCK

Pilots are superstitious and most have rituals they follow to make sure they return to base safely. For Broadside and his friend Matchstick, the good luck charm is to take turns agreeing to buy the drinks when they make it through each new Republic mission.

THIS GOLDEN DROID IS FLUENT in more than six million forms of communication and programmed for etiquette and protocol. He serves Padmé Amidala, the brave Senator from the planet Naboo.

C-3PO
MASTER OF PROTOCOL

Auditory sensors on side of head

Threepio is proud of his gold plating

Main power recharge socket

Midsection is lined with powerbus cables

DIPLOMACY

Long ago, C-3PO swore that they'd never get him aboard one of those dreadful starships, but now he's always accompanying Padmé on diplomatic missions. It can be dangerous, but it sure beats that dusty town on Tatooine. Now that was truly dreadful.

STATISTICS

SPECIES: Protocol droid
HEIGHT: 1.73 m (5 ft 8 in)
GENDER: Male programming
ALLEGIANCE: Republic
MANUFACTURER: Custom-built
WEAPONS: None
FEATURES: Programmed for diplomacy; fluent in more than six million forms of communication; knowledge of cultures and traditions
KNOWN COMPANIONS: Padmé Amidala, Anakin Skywalker, Obi-Wan Kenobi, Ahsoka Tano, Jar Jar Binks, R2-D2

A GUN-TOTING BOUNTY HUNTER FROM Duro, ruthless Cad Bane doesn't care what he's asked to do or who asks him to do it—he will do anything as long as he gets the credits that seem to be the only thing in the galaxy he loves.

Persuader blasters locked and loaded

MY ALLY IS THE BRAIN

Cad Bane has a healthy respect for the Jedi, having seen their abilities firsthand too many times. But he isn't intimidated by the Force. If anything, the Jedi are too quick to rely on it instead of thinking through their options. A smart bounty hunter can use the Jedi's faith in their powers to make them overconfident and careless.

Quick-draw holster of scuffed nerf-hide

STATISTICS

SPECIES: Duros

HEIGHT: 1.85 m (6 ft 1 in)

GENDER: Male

ALLEGIANCE: Himself

HOMEWORLD: Duro

WEAPONS: Twin custom Persuader blasters, bola, explosives, modified starfighter

TALENTS: Armed and unarmed combat; commanding network of bounty hunters

KNOWN COMPANIONS: Aurra Sing, Robonino, Shahan Alama, Todo 360, Cato Parasitti

Rocket boosters for quick escapes

THESE ENORMOUS INSECTS' gossamer wings allow them to fly at great speed and make hairpin turns in midair. Their curiosity sometimes attracts them to the buzz of passing aircraft, which they swarm after, mistaking the great machines for their own kind.

CAN-CELL
AERIAL ACROBAT

STATISTICS

SPECIES: Can-Cell
LENGTH: 3.35 m (11 ft)
HOMEWORLDS: Kashyyyk, Teth
ATTACKS: None
ECOLOGY: Can-Cells are speedy hunters and aerial acrobats

Gossamer wings allow fast flight

Compound eyes offer superb vision

Clawed feet grip and hold prey

RIDER TO THE RESCUE

On Teth, Asajj Ventress corners Ahsoka and R2-D2 on an empty landing platform. She moves to kill the Padawan, only to be interrupted by the arrival of Anakin Skywalker. R2-D2's imitation of a gunship's drone lures a Can-Cell near, and Anakin leaps onto the hunting fly's strong back to hitch a needed ride.

A MEMBER OF Coruscant's criminal underground, Cassie Cryar jumps at the chance to purchase a Jedi's stolen lightsaber. But the Terrelian bounty hunter soon learns that there's more to being a Jedi than just a laser blade.

Mask made of bone hides true features

LONG DROP

The nimble, quick Cassie Cryar is used to evading pursuit by racing over rooftops where others fear to follow. But she finds it hard to shake Ahsoka Tano. The Jedi chases Cassie across the skyline of Coruscant, with the occupants of passing speeders gaping in shock. All Ahsoka can think is: *Don't look down.*

Jedi weapon sought by anxious Padawan

CASSIE CRYAR
CORUSCANT BOUNTY HUNTER

STATISTICS

SPECIES: Terrelian Jango Jumper

HEIGHT: 1.82 m (6 ft)

GENDER: Female

ALLEGIANCE: Neutral

HOMEWORLD: Terrelia

WEAPONS: Stolen lightsaber

TALENTS: Combat training

KNOWN COMPANIONS:

Ione Marcy

Form-fitting boots allow easy movement

A SCRUFFY KLATOOINIAN BOUNTY hunter, Castas is part of Aurra Sing's crew during the Clone Wars. But when she tangles with the Republic Navy, Castas decides it's time for him to go his own way. Besides, he's tired of Aurra Sing telling him what to do all the time.

Blaster modified for longer range

Uniform stolen from unlucky officer

CASTAS
KLATOOINIAN GUN FOR HIRE

UNHAPPY EMPLOYEE

A bounty hunter is used to taking orders from just one person: himself. When hunters work together, someone —like Aurra Sing—has to be the boss and rewards have to be divided up. No self-respecting hunter can put up with such a situation for long.

STATISTICS

SPECIES: Klatooinian
HEIGHT: 1.99 m (6 ft 6 in)
GENDER: Male
ALLEGIANCE: Neutral
HOMEWORLD: Klatooine
WEAPONS: Customized blaster pistol
TALENTS: Combat; starship piloting
KNOWN COMPANIONS: Bossk, Aurra Sing, Boba Fett

Steel-toed boots with magnetic soles

CATO'S SHAPE-SHIFTING ABILITIES make her one of the galaxy's best spies and assassins. She proves useful to Cad Bane in his dangerous bid to steal a Holocron from the Jedi Temple, by sneaking Cato inside as a Jedi.

Helmet with night-vision lenses

Armor stolen from captured fugitive

Utility pouches hold odds and ends

Padding for swoop riding

CATO PARASITTI
CHANGELING SPY

STATISTICS

SPECIES: Clawdite
HEIGHT: 1.79 m (5 ft 10 in)
GENDER: Female
ALLEGIANCE: Neutral
HOMEWORLD: Zolan
WEAPONS: Underworld blaster rifle
TALENTS: Shapeshifting; infiltration
KNOWN COMPANIONS: Cad Bane, Todo 360

JEDI CHALLENGE

Cato Parasitti knows Cad Bane's reputation for ruthlessness all too well. But she isn't scared of him: A shapeshifter always has a way to blend into the crowd for a quick getaway. Besides, the idea of walking among Jedi disguised as one of their own is too tempting for Parasitti to resist.

A TWI'LEK FREEDOM FIGHTER, Cham leads the resistance against Ryloth's occupation by Separatists. He distrusts the Republic, seeing Ryloth's Senator Orn Free Taa as a corrupt politician and hopes to find a way to free Ryloth on his own.

Enlarged brain lobes process sensory input

CHAM SYNDULLA
REBEL OF RYLOTH

STATISTICS

SPECIES: Twi'lek
HEIGHT: 1.9 m (6 ft 3 in)
GENDER: Male
ALLEGIANCE: Twi'leks
HOMEWORLD: Ryloth
WEAPONS: Customized DL-44 blaster pistol, LL-30 blaster pistol
TALENTS: Blurrg riding; combat, recon and military expertise; leadership
KNOWN COMPANIONS: Gobi Glie, Tae Boon

Breastplate is a clan heirloom

GREATER GOOD

Cham is proud and hates the idea of working with a corrupt politician like Orn Free Taa. But his love for his planet is stronger than his pride, and so he agrees to talk with Taa and join forces with the Republic. Together, he hopes, his guerrillas and Mace Windu's troopers can defeat the evil Wat Tambor.

Trousers made of Jalavash worm silk

ONCE THE SENATOR FROM Naboo, Palpatine works tirelessly to keep the Republic intact amid a devastating war. He insists that he dislikes power and wishes only to see peace restored to the galaxy.

STATISTICS

SPECIES: Human
HEIGHT: 1.73 m (5 ft 8 in)
GENDER: Male
ALLEGIANCE: Republic
HOMEWORLD: Naboo
WEAPONS: None
TALENTS: Diplomacy; leadership; political strategy; ability to keep big secrets
KNOWN COMPANIONS: Mas Amedda, Orn Free Taa, Anakin Skywalker, Yoda

Palpatine is known for his gentle smile

Colorful but simple robes of office

CHANCELLOR PALPATINE
LEADER OF THE REPUBLIC

POWER CENTER

The glittering skyscrapers of Coruscant are Palpatine's arena—he is a very gifted politician, with the ability to change his tone from gentle and reasonable to firm and strong depending on the situation. Despite the terrors of the war with the Separatists, he remains enormously popular, and most in the galaxy trust him with their safety.

THE CHAIRMAN OF THE PANTORAN Assembly, Chi Cho has defended his home's interests for decades. He is enraged to find white-furred beings living on Orto Plutonia, an icy planet he regards as Pantora's property. He gives them a choice: Submit to Pantoran rule or die.

Pantoran military cap (with earmuffs)

Ornamental clasp fixes sash in place

CHI CHO
PANTORAN PARTISAN

TOUGH TALK

After making contact with the Talz, Obi-Wan Kenobi is hopeful a peaceful solution can be found, and arranges for them to meet the Pantorans. But to his dismay, Chairman Cho is determined to fight. The negotiations have failed, and war is near.

STATISTICS

SPECIES: Pantoran
HEIGHT: 1.98 m (6 ft 6 in)
GENDER: Male
ALLEGIANCE: Pantora
HOMEWORLD: Pantora
WEAPONS: Blaster pistol
TALENTS: Legal knowledge; leadership qualities
KNOWN COMPANIONS: Riyo Chuchi

Topcoat protects against bitter cold

STATISTICS

SPECIES: Human
HEIGHT: 1.83 m (6 ft)
GENDER: Male
ALLEGIANCE: Republic
HOMEWORLD: Kamino
WEAPONS: DC-15 blaster pistol
TALENTS: Trained for combat; skilled with machines
KNOWN COMPANIONS: Sergeant Slick, Gus, Hawk, Jester, Punch, Sketch

A SCARRED MEMBER OF SLICK'S squad, Chopper collects the fingers of fallen battle droids as grim trophies. That's weird—and against regulations. But it doesn't mean Chopper has betrayed his fellow clones to the Separatists.

Mismatched eyes from head injury

Necklace made of battle-droid fingers

CHOPPER
CLONE GONE BAD?

THE ACCUSED

Everyone in his squad knows Chopper is a bit strange. He seems to take war personally, gunning down battle droids with a scary mixture of joy and rage. Chopper lies about having visited the mess hall after the battle on Christophsis and Sgt. Slick seems ready to accuse him of treason. But Chopper has a question of his own: Where was Slick?

SOME CLONES WITH AN APTITUDE for machines are trained to service and maintain starfighters and gunships, supporting their brother pilots in the struggle against the Separatists. Before a battle, the decks of Republic carriers are abuzz with busy crews.

Direct link to flight deck

Utility vest holds tools and spare parts

CLONE FLIGHT CREW
STARFIGHTER SUPPORT

STATISTICS

SPECIES: Human
HEIGHT: 1.83 m (6 ft)
GENDER: Male
ALLEGIANCE: Republic
HOMEWORLD: Kamino
WEAPONS: None
EQUIPMENT: Diagnostic computers, astromech droids, mechanic's tools

CLEANING UP

A flight crew's work is never done! After a battle, it falls to them to refuel fighters, download flight reports, repair damage, and offload astromechs for servicing. Flight crews are trained to work quickly and quietly, ignoring any distraught pilots in their midst.

Noise insulation built into helmet

ALL CLONE TROOPERS ARE trained to fire artillery and starship turbolasers, but some clones are selected for further training and become experts at engaging enemies before they can reach close range.

Armor is reinforced against kick of guns

Gunner's armor pitted by flak and debris

STATISTICS

SPECIES: Human
HEIGHT: 1.83 m (6 ft)
GENDER: Male
ALLEGIANCE: Republic
HOMEWORLD: Kamino
WEAPONS: DC-15 blaster pistol
EQUIPMENT: None

CLONE GUNNER
SEPS IN THEIR SIGHTS

HOLD STEADY

The hardest lesson for a gunner to learn is really about forgetting: To man a heavy gun effectively, a gunner must not think about the fact that every shot he fires gives his enemies another chance to figure out his location and make him a target.

CLONE MEDICAL OFFICERS ARE specially trained in healing, working alongside surgical droids to treat the injured in medical centers located far from the front lines. It takes tough clones to help wounded men who have the same face they do.

Badge indicates medical speciality

CLONE MEDICAL OFFICER
CARING FOR AN ARMY

Officer's uniform in medical colors

STATISTICS

SPECIES: Human
HEIGHT: 1.83 m (6 ft)
GENDER: Male
ALLEGIANCE: Republic
HOMEWORLD: Kamino
WEAPONS: None
EQUIPMENT: Datapads, medical supplies

KALIIDA ASSAULT

The Kaliida Shoals medical center treats clones wounded all across the Outer Rim. Its location is top secret, but General Grievous discovers it and rushes to destroy it. Nala Se's medical officers remain at their posts, hoping the dreaded warlord can be stopped.

STATISTICS

SPECIES: Human
HEIGHT: 1.83 m (6 ft)
GENDER: Male
ALLEGIANCE: Republic
HOMEWORLD: Kamino
WEAPONS: DC-15
blaster pistol
EQUIPMENT:
Comlink,
code cylinder

THE TOP OFFICERS OF the Republic military are non-clones, but some clones have received special training in military strategy. They fill out the lower officer ranks and are a common sight on starship bridges.

Rank badge
of Republic
military

Datapad used by
officers on the go

Gloves are
worn as
military
tradition

CLONE OFFICER
DIRECTING THEIR BROTHERS

DUTY CALLS

Clone officers in the Republic army sometimes serve "out of armor" to improve certain skills or while recuperating from injuries suffered on the battlefield. At Abregado, Commander Wolffe is on such a duty rotation when General Grievous's *Malevolence* attacks the Jedi Cruiser *Triumphant*.

ONE OF THE MORE DANGEROUS jobs in the Republic military is to defuse bombs. Clones who perform this vital task must have a gentle touch, steady nerves, and a sense of how machines work. And they must do their job while ignoring the whine of blaster fire around them.

CLONE ORDNANCE SPECIALIST
EASY DOES IT!

STATISTICS

SPECIES: Human
HEIGHT: 1.83 m (6 ft)
GENDER: Male
ALLEGIANCE: Republic
HOMEWORLD: Kamino
WEAPONS: DC-15 blaster pistol
EQUIPMENT: Explosives sensors, ion probes, defusing tools

Insignia reserved for bomb squad

Virus-laden bomb set to explode

GIFTS FROM DR. VINDI

Hidden below the surface of Naboo is Dr. Nuvo Vindi's lab containing bombs filled with the deadly Blue Shadow Virus. The troopers of the bomb squad know the stakes have never been higher: If the virus escapes the lab, it could end all life in the galaxy.

CLONE PILOTS CAN FLY ANYTHING, from gunships and assault shuttles to starfighters. Their superb reflexes and quick wits make them a "breed apart" among the clones serving the Republic. They protect troopers and engage Separatists in space.

Pilot's helmet includes improved sensors

Sensors measure pilot's vital signs

STATISTICS

SPECIES: Human
HEIGHT: 1.83 m (6 ft)
GENDER: Male
ALLEGIANCE: Republic
HOMEWORLD: Kamino
WEAPONS: DC-15 blaster pistol
EQUIPMENT: Survival gear, communications equipment

HEADS UP!

The life of a pilot is full of dangers. In space, vulture droids and Separatist warships want to shoot you down. In the atmosphere, vultures are joined by droids blasting away at you with ground-based artillery. And sometimes, airborne visitors arrive to do battle at disturbingly close range.

GENETICALLY IDENTICAL warriors designed, grown, and trained by the Kaminoans, clone troopers defend the Republic by the millions, battling the Separatists' droid army on thousands of war-torn worlds.

CLONE TROOPER
THE SOLDIERS OF THE REPUBLIC

Helmet features antenna and breath filter

STATISTICS

SPECIES: Human
HEIGHT: 1.83 m (6 ft)
GENDER: Male
ALLEGIANCE: Republic
HOMEWORLD: Kamino
WEAPONS: DC-15 blaster pistol, DC-15 blaster rifle
EQUIPMENT: Plastoid-alloy armor, body glove, comlink, survival gear, grappling hook, macrobinoculars

Troopers train with many weapons

Armor includes twenty lightweight plates

A SENSE OF DUTY

Clone troopers spend their lives surrounded by fellow soldiers with their own face and they develop strong bonds that make them very effective in battle. However, they have been trained to complete missions at all costs and accept that many of them will die in combat.

Exhaust vent for suit coolant

BATTLE DROIDS don't fear fire, but most of their living opponents do. Swarming foes such as Geonosians can overwhelm clones with blasters, but think twice when they hear the hiss of flamethrowers. Flame-trooper squads prove critical in the assault on Geonosis.

Two-handed grip required for weapon

STATISTICS

SPECIES: Human

HEIGHT: 1.83 m (6 ft)

GENDER: Male

ALLEGIANCE: Republic

HOMEWORLD: Kamino

WEAPONS: BlasTech X-42 flamethrower, DC-15 blaster pistol

EQUIPMENT: Plastoid-alloy armor, flame-retardant body glove, comlink

Insulated body glove is flame-retardant

MEN IN FIRE

Flame troopers are specially trained to resist humans' natural instinct to move away from fire, particularly in enclosed places such as Geonosis's catacombs. Insulated suits and flame-retardant gear help keep flame troopers safer while they go about their dangerous business.

CC-2224, OR "COMMANDER CODY," leads the 212th Attack Battalion, and is Obi-Wan Kenobi's second-in-command. A cautious but highly capable soldier, he and Rex have become close friends over a number of missions.

Secondary antenna for communications

CODY
LEADER OF THE 212TH

SIDE BY SIDE

Few Jedi and clone officers develop a bond as close as the one between Obi-Wan Kenobi and Commander Cody. Engagements at places such as Ryloth, Black Stall Station, and Geonosis have taught Cody to respect Obi-Wan's skill as a warrior, and Obi-Wan has come to trust that Cody will never let him down.

STATISTICS

SPECIES: Human

HEIGHT: 1.83 m (6 ft)

GENDER: Male

ALLEGIANCE: Republic

HOMEWORLD: Kamino

WEAPONS: DC-17 pistols, DC-15 blaster rifle

TALENTS: Armed and unarmed combat; jetpack expertise; knowledge of recon and military tactics; leadership

KNOWN COMPANIONS: Obi-Wan Kenobi, Captain Rex, Boil, Waxer

Specialized anti-glare visor

STATISTICS

SPECIES: Battle droid
HEIGHT: 1.91 m (6 ft 3 in)
GENDER: Male programming
ALLEGIANCE: Separatists
MANUFACTURER: Baktoid
WEAPONS: E-5 blaster rifle, thermal detonator, stun baton, vibrosword
EQUIPMENT: Laser cutters, electrobinoculars, speech modulator

REPUBLIC FORCES LIKE TO mock B1 battle droids as "clankers," as they are dumb and easily defeated. But no one mocks commando droids—they are faster, tougher, smarter, and programmed for stealth missions and speed.

Markings denote high rank

Reinforced droid armor plating

Midsection is tough and flexible

COST OF WAR

Commando droids are made for missions that ordinary battle droids would make a mess of, and clone troopers have learned to fear them. Fortunately, there aren't many of these units: They are much more expensive than the B1 battle droids to produce, maintain, and reprogram.

COMMANDO DROID
A BETTER BATTLE DROID

THE PUBLIC LEADER of the Separatists, Dooku left the Jedi and fell to the dark side of the Force. He bears the name Darth Tyranus, and obeys the orders of his mysterious Master, known as Darth Sidious.

COUNT DOOKU
FALLEN JEDI

Imposing stare frightens servants

DESERT DUEL

On Geonosis, Count Dooku gave young Anakin Skywalker a bitter lesson in the Jedi arts, cutting the reckless Padawan's arm from his body. Crossing sabers with him again on Tatooine, Dooku is impressed by how much the boy has grown—and by the anger Anakin can barely hold inside.

STATISTICS

SPECIES: Human
HEIGHT: 1.93 m (6 ft 4 in)
GENDER: Male
ALLEGIANCE: Sith
HOMEWORLD: Serenno
WEAPONS: Lightsaber
TALENTS: Dark side abilities; Makashi lightsaber combat; leadership
KNOWN COMPANIONS:
Asajj Ventress, General Grievous, Darth Sidious, Wat Tambor, Nute Gunray

Cloak woven by artisans on Vjun

Curved Sith lightsaber

STATISTICS

SPECIES: Battle droid
LENGTH: 1.49 m (4 ft 11in)
GENDER: None
ALLEGIANCE: Separatists
MANUFACTURER: Techno Union
WEAPONS: Twin blasters
EQUIPMENT: Jet sprayer,
vacuum pump

NICKNAMED "MUCKRACKERS" BY clone troops, these droids use their four legs to move effectively through muddy, swampy terrain. Veteran clones know to avoid their guns by leaping on top of them. These droids come in various sizes, specialized for different missions.

CRAB DROID
SEPARATIST WAR MACHINE

SWAMP SOLDIERS

On Rodia, C-3PO and Jar Jar Binks encounter crab droids prowling the hangars on orders from Nute Gunray. The monstrous droids are a perfect fit for Rodia's swamps and shallow lagoons, hiding in the water before scrambling ashore to back up squads of battle droids carrying out Gunray's commands.

Duranium arms can pierce rock

Stalks house sensory gear

Deadly twin blasters on undercarriage

A DESERTER FROM THE CLONE trooper ranks, Cut Lawquane has sought to make a new life for himself on a Saleucami farm. He wants only to live in peace, but must fight when commando droids attack his home.

Some clones have receding hairlines

CUT LAWQUANE
CLONE DESERTER

STATISTICS

SPECIES: Human
HEIGHT: 1.83 m (6 ft)
GENDER: Male
ALLEGIANCE: Neutral
HOMEWORLD: Kamino
WEAPONS: DC-15 blaster pistol, DC-15 blaster rifle
TALENTS: Trained for combat, recon, and military tactics; knowledge of farming
KNOWN COMPANIONS: Suu Lawquane, Shaeeah Lawquane, Jek Lawquane

Ancient rifle owned by Suu Lawquane

Wrappings keep dirt out of boot tops

SECRETS REVEALED?

The arrival of Captain Rex on Cut and Suu's farm forces the clone deserter to face a day he hoped would never arrive. What will Cut tell his children about the war and the role that he played in it?

THE DARK LORD OF THE Sith, Sidious is the puppeteer behind the terrible Clone Wars, manipulating events through his apprentice, Count Dooku. Many doubt he exists, but Sidious is all too real, and his plots threaten to plunge the entire galaxy into a new age of Sith darkness.

Cowl hides face from his agents

Sidious's true identity is known to few

Black robes hide Sidious from sight

STATISTICS

SPECIES: Human
HEIGHT: 1.73 m (5 ft 8 in)
GENDER: Male
ALLEGIANCE: Sith
HOMEWORLD: Naboo
WEAPONS: Lightsaber
TALENTS: Master of the dark side; knowledge of Sith traditions; manipulating events
KNOWN COMPANIONS: Count Dooku, General Grievous, Nute Gunray

DARTH SIDIOUS

HIDDEN SITH MASTER

DARK FUTURE

After his plot to steal Jedi children succeeds, Sidious gives the nanny droid RO-Z67 orders via holocam. He hopes his evil experiments will produce an army of dark siders to help him control the galaxy.

A BUREAUCRAT SERVING THE Republic's Ministry of Intelligence, Davu Golec makes for an unlikely hero. But when he finds out that evidence is being faked to justify war with Mandalore, he risks his life to help Duchess Satine uncover the truth.

Skepticism about quality of data

Data card contains unaltered transmission

DAVU GOLEC
SHARER OF SECRETS

STATISTICS

SPECIES: Human
HEIGHT: 1.93 m (6 ft 4 in)
GENDER: Male
ALLEGIANCE: Republic
HOMEWORLD: Coruscant
WEAPONS: None
TALENTS: Bureaucracy; data-slicing
KNOWN COMPANIONS: Duchess Satine

Uniform of Intelligence Ministry

RIGHT & WRONG

Davu knows not everything in war is quite the way politicians say it is. But someone within the Republic has edited a Mandalorian transmission to change its meaning—and people will die because of it. Davu brings the unedited tape to Satine, hoping she can prevent a tragic loss of life.

A VETERAN CLONE TROOPER, Denal has seen action from Ruusan and Tatooine to Rodia and Devaron. Captain Rex has come to rely on him, trusting his experience and instincts on any number of missions against Separatist forces.

Blue markings of 501st unit

DC-15 held in ready position

DENAL
VETERAN OF THE 501ST

STATISTICS

SPECIES: Human

HEIGHT: 1.83 m (6 ft)

GENDER: Male

ALLEGIANCE: Republic

HOMEWORLD: Kamino

WEAPONS: DC-15 blaster pistol, DC-15 blaster rifle

TALENTS: Combat, recon, and military tactics; jetpack expertise

KNOWN COMPANIONS: Captain Rex, Anakin Skywalker, Ahsoka Tano

CLOSE RANGE

Above Devaron, Denal confronts Cad Bane, and then a figure in Denal's 501st armor limps aboard the last shuttle to escape the doomed ship. But the trooper is leaking green blood! It's not Denal but Cad Bane, wearing Denal's stolen armor.

SOMETIMES CALLED DROIDEKAS or "rollies," these three-legged droids are among the toughest Separatist units. Even Jedi fall back when faced with destroyer droids' energy shields and powerful cannons, calling in artillery strikes or seeking a stealthy avenue for attack.

STATISTICS

SPECIES: Battle droid
HEIGHT: 1.83 m (6 ft)
GENDER: None
ALLEGIANCE: Separatists
MANUFACTURER: Colicoids
WEAPONS: Twin blaster cannons
EQUIPMENT: Shield projector, radiation sensors

DESTROYER DROID
ROLLING DEATH

Primary sensor antenna

Twin high-energy laser cannon

Deflector shield projector plate

Foot claw for hard surfaces

ATTACK STANCE

A droideka unfolds with smooth, easy grace: It effortlessly uncurls, snaps onto its trio of legs, lifts its head, extends its arms, and encases itself in a blue globe of protective energy. You might even call it a beautiful sight—except few survive an up-close look at it.

Translucent skin seems to glow

ONCE CONSIDERED THE stuff of tall tales told by spacers, the Diathim are actually real and they dwell on the moon Millius Prime. The Separatists drove them from their home, leaving them marooned on forlorn Iego, where their bedraggled beauty is a reminder of better days.

STATISTICS

SPECIES: Diathim
HEIGHT: 2.35 m (7 ft 9 in)
HOMEWORLD: Millius Prime

DIATHIM
ANGEL OF IEGO

Wings shimmer in the moonlight

ANGELIC MESSAGE

Obi-Wan is amazed to find himself speaking with a being out of a children's fairy tale. But the angel he meets on Iego is very real. What she tells him provides the knowledge he needs on how to escape the planet and destroy the Separatist defense network there.

THE LEADER OF MALASTARE'S Dugs, Doge Urus controls fuel reserves crucial to the Republic in its fight against the Separatists. The wily Dug leader seeks to exploit this strength when he negotiates a treaty with Coruscant.

DOGE NAKHA URUS
DUG NOBILITY

Shrewd gaze sizes up rivals

Leg straps of rich leather

Dugs run with surprising speed

TOUGH TALK

Doge Urus seems to support a treaty between Malastare's Dugs and the Republic. But the Dug leader is worried about the damage done to his planet by the fighting, and he senses how desperate Palpatine is to secure Malastare's fuel for his armed forces. What Dug passes up a chance to take advantage?

DUTIFUL DIGGERS

Dwarf spider droids were originally built by the feared Commerce Guild to attack renegade miners behind barricades deep underground. The Separatists have built on the original design by creating larger models armed with laser cannons that offer much greater punch in battle.

High quality signal antenna

Photoreceptors see in infrared

Primary laser cannon

Clawed feet can climb up cliffs

DWARF SPIDER DROID
METAL MASCOT

STATISTICS

SPECIES: Battle droid

HEIGHT: 1.98 m (6 ft 6 in)

GENDER: Male programming

ALLEGIANCE: Separatists

MANUFACTURER: Baktoid

WEAPONS: Heavy blaster cannon

EQUIPMENT: Infrared photoreceptors, clawed feet

A ROOKIE TROOPER WITH AN eye for detail and a sense of calm, Echo isn't troubled by the lack of excitement on the Rishi Moon. He's content to read manuals and work to improve the skills he'll need as a soldier fighting for the Republic.

Sense of calm bodes well for promotions

Handprint made in Rishi eel blood

ECHO
AN EYE FOR DETAIL

STATISTICS

SPECIES: Human
HEIGHT: 1.83 m (6 ft)
GENDER: Male
ALLEGIANCE: Republic
HOMEWORLD: Kamino
WEAPONS: DC-15 blaster pistol, DC-15 blaster rifle
TALENTS: Combat, recon, and military tactics
KNOWN COMPANIONS: Sergeant O'Niner, Fives, Cutup, Hevy

Armor is no longer shiny after combat

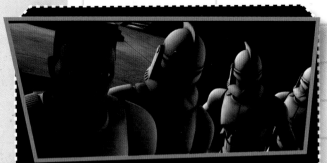

ON THEIR OWN

Echo (CT-21-0408) never dreamed his skills would be needed quite so soon: Commando droids invade the Rishi Moon base, killing O'Niner and several troopers. Echo, Cutup, Fives, and Hevy must stay calm if they are to stop the Separatists.

THIS JEDI COUNCIL MEMBER narrowly survived death when his gunship was shot down during the Battle of Geonosis. But, overwhelmed by Grievous's droids, Eeth is taken captive.

Zabraks have vestigial horns

Armor battered from combat

Eeth favors long, loose robes

EETH KOTH
JEDI SURVIVOR

STATISTICS

SPECIES: Zabrak
HEIGHT: 1.71 m (5 ft 7 in)
GENDER: Male
ALLEGIANCE: Jedi Order
HOMEWORLD: Nar Shaddaa
WEAPONS: Lightsaber
TALENTS: Force-sensitivity
KNOWN COMPANIONS:
Mace Windu, Yoda,
Ki-Adi-Mundi, Adi Gallia,
Plo Koon

TOO MANY

Jedi Knights are superbly trained as warriors, and the members of the Jedi Council represent the best of the Order. But even they aren't invincible. When Grievous invades Koth's cruiser with a squad of MagnaGuards and commando droids, not even Eeth can prevail.

A MEMBER OF SUGI'S BAND of mercenaries, proud Embo defends a village of Felucian farmers against pirate attacks. He's not happy when a group of Jedi arrive and threaten to take his job away— and accuse him of exploiting the villagers he has agreed to protect.

EMBO
WARRIOR FOR HIRE

Kyuzo war helmet used as both shield and weapon

Fingers are strong and dextrous

EMBO'S PRIDE

The Jedi seem to doubt that Embo and his three fellow bounty hunters can defend a village against an entire pirate band. But Embo is determined to prove them wrong: They've never seen what a fully trained Kyuzo warrior can do—particularly a Kyuzo warrior who feels his honor has been questioned.

Rich kama has seen better days

STATISTICS

SPECIES: Kyuzo
HEIGHT: 1.99 m (6 ft 6 in)
GENDER: Male
ALLEGIANCE: Neutral
HOMEWORLD: Phatrong
WEAPONS: Bowcaster
TALENTS: Expert at armed and unarmed combat
KNOWN COMPANIONS: Sugi, Seripas, Rumi Paramita

CC-3714, NICKNAMED "FIL," SERVES under the young Jedi Nahdar Vebb, aiding the inexperienced Mon Calamari in several pitched battles. His squad is assigned to a strike mission in the Vassek system, aimed at recapturing Nute Gunray.

Polarized T-visor reduces glare

STATISTICS

SPECIES: Human
HEIGHT: 1.83 m (6 ft)
GENDER: Male
ALLEGIANCE: Republic
HOMEWORLD: Kamino
WEAPONS: DC-17 pistols, DC-15 blaster rifle
TALENTS: Armed and unarmed combat; recon and military tactics; leadership
KNOWN COMPANIONS:
Kit Fisto, Nahdar Vebb

Twin pistols held at the ready

KILLED IN ACTION

Commander Fil knows that a hideaway used by General Grievous will be full of traps, but not even the veteran clone is prepared for an attack by a savage roggwart. Fil is killed by a blow from the beast's tail, leaving a furious Nahdar to promise that he will be avenged.

THESE BATTLE DROIDS HAVE been pressed into fighting fires on Separatist warships. They have been programmed to use special firefighting gear and identify the best tactics for coping with emergencies in deep space.

Red badge indicates emergency role

FIREFIGHTER DROID
WARSHIP GUARDIAN

Standard backpack altered to hold firefighting gear

STATISTICS

SPECIES: Battle droid

HEIGHT: 1.91 m (6 ft 3 in)

GENDER: Male programming

ALLEGIANCE: Separatists

MANUFACTURER: Baktoid

WEAPONS: None

EQUIPMENT: Firefighting gear

Control for hose aperture and flow

Yellow markings for visibility in smoke

Tough material resists heat

HANGAR FIRE

After the Nubian yacht carrying Padmé Amidala and C-3PO crashes in a hangar aboard the *Malevolence*, firefighter droids rush to put out the flames before they can spread elsewhere in the ship, leaving the pursuit and capture of the fugitives to battle droids designed and equipped for combat operations.

Bicep plate allows arm movement

Neck seal between helmet and body glove

FIVES
TATTOOED TROOPER

Backup comlink and suit controls

STATISTICS

SPECIES: Human

HEIGHT: 1.83 m (6 ft)

GENDER: Male

ALLEGIANCE: Republic

HOMEWORLD: Kamino

WEAPONS: DC-15 blaster pistol, DC-15 blaster rifle

TALENTS: Trained for combat, recon, and military tactics

KNOWN COMPANIONS: Sergeant O'Niner, Echo, Hevy

SURVIVORS

By sacrificing his life, Hevy spoils the Separatist plan to invade Kamino, saving his fellow clones. Having seen battle, Fives and his troopers are no longer "shinies."

CC-1010, NAMED "FOX," IS A commander in the Coruscant Guard, far from the front lines. But when Padmé Amidala is kidnapped in Coruscant's lower levels, he realizes Separatist threats are everywhere.

FOX
GUARDING CORUSCANT

Symbol of the Galactic Senate

FOX ON THE RUN

Fox's duties have made him familiar with the seedier levels of Coruscant, including the palace of the foul crimelord Ziro the Hutt. When word comes that Ziro has imprisoned a Republic Senator, Fox and his Guardsmen rush to the scene.

Quick-draw holster for DC-17s

Greaves decorated in Guard colors

STATISTICS

SPECIES: Human
HEIGHT: 1.83 m (6 ft)
GENDER: Male
ALLEGIANCE: Republic
HOMEWORLD: Kamino
WEAPONS: DC-17 pistols, DC-15 blaster rifle, DC-15 blaster pistol
TALENTS: Trained in armed and unarmed combat; recon tactics; sniper training; leadership
KNOWN COMPANIONS: Commander Stone, Obi-Wan Kenobi, Padmé Amidala

STATISTICS

SPECIES: Kaleesh cyborg
HEIGHT: 2.16 m (7 ft 1 in)
GENDER: Male
ALLEGIANCE: Separatists
HOMEWORLD: Kalee
WEAPONS: Lightsabers,
E-5 blaster rifle
TALENTS: Lightsaber
combat;
knowledge
of military
tactics; starship piloting
KNOWN COMPANIONS: Count
Dooku, A4-D, Gor, Nute
Gunray, Gha Nachkt

ONCE A KALEESH WARLORD, GRIEVOUS is now more machine than flesh, with lightsaber skills that make him the equal of a Jedi. He hates the Jedi and takes the sabers of those he kills for grim trophies. The cyborg loathes droids, and flies into a rage if he is mistaken for mechanical.

GENERAL GRIEVOUS
STEEL WARLORD

Organic eyes remain after modifications

Armorplast shielding hides living organs

JEDI DUEL

On Vassek's moon, Grievous finds Count Dooku has set a trap to test his abilities: His guards have been deactivated, and Jedi are loose inside his secret lair. No matter: Grievous kills Nahdar Vebb quickly, and proves eager to cross lightsabers with Kit Fisto.

Magnetized talons of durasteel

GEONOSIANS TYPICALLY DEFEAT their enemies through sheer numbers. They are also cunning opponents, whether armed with blasters or piloting speedy starfighters. Clone troopers have learned to respect this warrior caste.

STATISTICS

SPECIES: Geonosian
HEIGHT: 1.7 m (5 ft 7 in)
GENDER: Male
ALLEGIANCE: Separatists
HOMEWORLD: Geonosis
WEAPONS: Force pike, sonic blaster
EQUIPMENT: Wings, chitin armor

GEONOSIAN
HIVE HORROR

Soldier drones can fly or hover

Geonosians can eat almost anything

DEFENDING THE HIVE

Geonosians are smart fighters, but think nothing of sacrificing themselves when against impossible odds. Drones are only faintly aware of themselves as individuals. To them, the survival of the hive is the only thing that matters, and if told to die for it, they will do so without hesitation.

Oscillators produce devastating sonic ball

Claws let drones hang upside down

PROFESSIONAL SCAVENGERS LIKE Gha Nachkt are quick to arrive after space battles, scouring debris fields for droids, weapons, and starship parts that they can repair and sell. Nachkt makes his big score at Bothawui when he finds R2-D2 amid the debris, his droid brain still intact.

Ugly features hide a keen mind

Fingernails badly in need of clipping

GHA NACHKT
SPACE SCAVENGER

STATISTICS

SPECIES: Trandoshan

HEIGHT: 1.75 m (5 ft 9 in)

GENDER: Male

ALLEGIANCE: Neutral

HOMEWORLD: Trandosha

WEAPONS: Ion prod

TALENTS: Starship piloting and repairs; droid programming

KNOWN COMPANIONS: General Grievous, Wat Tambor, IG-86 assassin droids

SOME REWARD

Gha Nachkt realizes the military secrets in R2-D2's memory are worth a fortune to the Separatist war machine, and thinks he deserves a bonus for his discovery. And indeed, Grievous has something special in store for him.

Smelly feet are legendary

69

CHAM SYNDULLA'S RESISTANCE CELL has many warriors, but also draws strength from Gobi Glie's talents as a minstrel. His songs not only celebrate Syndulla's deeds, but also rally the rebels in their fight for a free Ryloth.

Excellent ears for melody

Lekku help Twi'leks store memories

GOBI GLIE
TWI'LEK BARD

STATISTICS

SPECIES: Twi'lek
HEIGHT: 1.84 m (6 ft)
GENDER: Male
ALLEGIANCE: Cham Syndulla
HOMEWORLD: Ryloth
WEAPONS: LL-30 blaster pistol
TALENTS: Musical ability
KNOWN COMPANIONS: Cham Syndulla, Tae Boon

Kneepads for work in blurrg pens

GET WELL SOON

Cham Syndulla's fighters hide in Ryloth's badlands, far from medical care. When Mace Windu visits Syndulla's camp, Gobi Glie is still recovering from an arm injury suffered in a skirmish with battle droids. But he will be back fighting soon: He knows Cham and his planet need him.

STATISTICS

SPECIES: Roggwart
HEIGHT: 4.5 m (14 ft 9 in)
GENDER: Male
ALLEGIANCE: General Grievous
HOMEWORLD: Guiteica
WEAPONS: Mechanical arms, sharp teeth
TALENTS: Great strength; trained to keep watch
KNOWN COMPANIONS: General Grievous, A4-D

ROGGWARTS ARE NATIVE TO Guiteica, and many Kaleesh keep the beasts as pets and guardians. Gor keeps vicious watch over Grievous's Vassek lair, and the cyborg general treats the great beast like a beloved pet.

Mechanical arms attached by A4-D

GOR
MONSTROUS PET

Slashing claws can retract

Powerful leg muscles

Tail can impale attackers

IMPROVEMENTS

Roggwarts are ferocious creatures in their natural state, but Grievous sees a way to improve Gor as a guardian, just as he has improved himself through the addition of cybernetic limbs and thick armor. With A4-D's help, Grievous augments Gor with an exoskeleton, armor, and new mechanical arms.

CC-1004, NICKNAMED COMMANDER "Gree," commands the 41st Elite Corps, led by the Jedi General Luminara Unduli. His nickname reflects his interest in alien cultures, which he studies in hopes of learning new lessons about military strategy.

GREE
LUMINARA'S RIGHT HAND

Thermal detonator

Bandolier holds extra ammo

Kneeplates need frequent replacement

NUTE'S JAILER
Aboard the *Tranquility*, Commander Gree assists Captain Argyus with guarding the captive Nute Gunray—and finds himself in hand-to-hand combat with the Senate commando when Argyus shoots his own men and is revealed as a Separatist agent.

IN THE CAVES of Vanqor, Obi-Wan and Anakin accidentally trespass on the turf of a tribe of gundarks—and find they must fight for their lives against the beasts. Varieties of gundarks are found on several different planets.

GUNDARK
BIG, TOUGH, AND MEAN

RUN!

Jedi Knights are tough, but gundarks might be tougher—particularly when they're defending their nests. Anakin and Obi-Wan pursue Count Dooku to Vanqor, only to find themselves in a gundark tribe's cave. With his lightsaber lost, Anakin finds the best defense isn't using the Force, but a much older, simpler strategy: Run as fast as you can!

Gundark breath is best avoided

Small arms secure prey

Big arms are used for running and fighting

Front legs end in digging claws

STATISTICS

SPECIES: Gundark
HEIGHT: 2.5 m (8 ft 2 in)
HOMEWORLD: Vanqor, others
WEAPONS: Fierce bite, tearing arms
ECOLOGY: Gundarks are powerful four-armed beasts with big ears and bad dispositions

A MEMBER OF Sergeant Slick's squad, Gus falls under suspicion as a possible traitor. But the clone is able to clear his name: He was wounded and being tended to by a medical droid at the Republic base. The guilty party is someone else.

Rakish goatee is carefully tended

GUS
WOUNDED WARRIOR

STATISTICS

SPECIES: Human
HEIGHT: 1.83 m (6 ft)
GENDER: Male
ALLEGIANCE: Republic
HOMEWORLD: Kamino
WEAPONS: DC-15 blaster pistol, DC-15 blaster rifle
TALENTS: Trained for combat, recon, and military tactics
KNOWN COMPANIONS: Sergeant Slick, Chopper, Hawk, Jester, Punch, Sketch

Plastoid armor covers black body glove

FRONT LINES

Christophsis is a vital world to the Republic war effort because it is rich in minerals and is on a strategic trade route in the Outer Rim. Gus is just one of many brave clones who stand against the Separatists' metal legions in a pitched battle that devastates Christophsis's beautiful crystalline cities.

Combat training received on Kamino

STATISTICS

SPECIES: Gutkurr

HEIGHT: 2 m (6 ft 7 in)

HOMEWORLD: Ryloth

WEAPONS: Sharp teeth

ECOLOGY: Gutkurrs dig into the desert sands with their clawed limbs and wait for prey to pass overhead

THE SEPARATISTS OCCUPYING Ryloth starve these fierce, two-legged desert predators and then release them to hunt Twi'lek fugitives. The creatures track down the defenseless Twi'leks with their long strides and devour them with a few snaps of their terrible fanged jaws.

Thick shell protects internal organs

Compound eyes can find prey in low light

GUTKURR
TERROR OF RYLOTH

Powerful claws are used for digging

NABAT PERIL

In an effort to thin the clones' ranks, tactical droid TX-20 releases gutkurrs that he's starved until they are mad with hunger. The predators race from their cages to find food, and manage to kill a number of Ghost Company's troopers in their attack. But TX-20 hasn't imagined that a Jedi's powers include soothing savage beasts: Obi-Wan Kenobi calms the gutkurrs and traps them.

A RUTHLESS PIRATE, GWARM swaggers into the Felucian village of Akira as if he owns it, demanding that the villagers turn over their healing herb crop. When the villagers have other ideas, bullying Gwarm is ready for a fight.

Vibro-ax lashed to rifle barrel

Typical leathery Weequay skin

Sniper scope for hitting far-off targets

GWARM
FELUCIAN RAIDER

STATISTICS

SPECIES: Weequay
HEIGHT: 1.92 m (6 ft 6 in)
GENDER: Male
ALLEGIANCE: Hondo Ohnaka
HOMEWORLD: Florrum
WEAPONS: Underworld blaster rifle
TALENTS: Combat; sniper skills; intimidation
KNOWN COMPANIONS: Hondo Ohnaka

THE PRICE OF NYSILLIM

Gwarm is a lieutenant to the infamous Outer Rim pirate Hondo Ohnaka, who's been trying to become a player in the rich black market for healing herbs. On Felucia, Gwarm discovers a potentially big score: The farmers of Akira grow nysillim, one of the galaxy's most valuable crops.

SENATOR HALLE BURTONI represents Kamino, the birthplace of the Republic's clone army and an influential planet. She pushes the Senate to vote for more clone production, hoping to enrich her homeworld, and she opposes Senators working to reduce military spending.

Kaminoans like simple jewelry

Cloak indicates Senatorial status

STATISTICS

SPECIES: Kaminoan
HEIGHT: 2.13 m (7 ft)
GENDER: Female
ALLEGIANCE: Republic
HOMEWORLD: Kamino
WEAPONS: None
TALENTS: Diplomacy; legislative strategy
KNOWN COMPANIONS: Mee Deechi, C-069, Orn Free Taa, Padmé Amidala

HALLE BURTONI
TOWERING POWER BROKER

THE BUSINESS OF WARFARE

Halle Burtoni sees the Senate's advocates of peace as dangerously naïve—the forces of Count Dooku are interested only in the destruction of the Republic. With the help of Senators such as her ally Mee Deechi, Halle works tirelessly to keep credits pouring into the Kaminoans' coffers.

Brightly polished walking cane

AN EXPERT PILOT, HAWK HAS seen action on many worlds, including the extraction of clone troopers from dangerous fighting on the war-torn world of Christophsis and setting down in the jungles of Teth to offload a strike force.

Bird of prey adorns scarred helmet

HAWK
CHRISTOPHSIS PILOT

STATISTICS

SPECIES: Human

HEIGHT: 1.83 m (6 ft)

GENDER: Male

ALLEGIANCE: Republic

HOMEWORLD: Kamino

WEAPONS: DC-15 blaster pistol

TALENTS: Expert starfighter pilot; combat training; knowledge of military tactics

KNOWN COMPANIONS: Anakin Skywalker, Obi-Wan Kenobi, Ahsoka Tano, Captain Rex

Fitted armor over body glove

TARGET: TETH

Hawk's seen enough battles to know that Teth is going to be a bad one: The Republic gunships must bring squads of clone troopers all the way to the jungle floor, then return to pick them up from the mesas high above, all while under heavy fire from prowling vulture droids.

HELIOS-3D IS ONE OF THREE IG-86 droids used by Cad Bane in his daring assault on the Senate. 3D's task is to drive the airspeeder transporting Ziro the Hutt from the detention center back to the Senate building, ignoring the insults hurled by his angry Hutt master.

E-5 blaster used in close quarters

Symbol of Ziro the Hutt's organization

Durasteel limbs designed for heavy gravity

STATISTICS

SPECIES: IG-86 sentinel droid
HEIGHT: 1.99 m (6 ft 6 in)
GENDER: Male programming
ALLEGIANCE: Neutral
MANUFACTURER: Holowan Mechanicals
WEAPONS: Underworld blaster rifle, E-5 blaster rifle
TALENTS: Combat; knowledge of military tactics; sensor suite
KNOWN COMPANIONS: Cad Bane, Aurra Sing, Robonino, Shahan Alama

HELIOS-3D
SENATE INVADER

ORN'S DRIVER

The hostage crisis gripping the Senate is bad enough, but it gets worse for Orn Free Taa when he learns that he'll have to ride to the Judiciary Detention Center in an airspeeder driven by an armed, pitiless assassin droid.

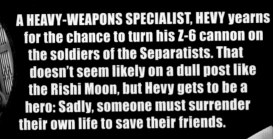

A HEAVY-WEAPONS SPECIALIST, HEVY yearns for the chance to turn his Z-6 cannon on the soldiers of the Separatists. That doesn't seem likely on a dull post like the Rishi Moon, but Hevy gets to be a hero: Sadly, someone must surrender their own life to save their friends.

Determination to defeat the enemy

Shoulder "bell" allows movement

HEVY
HERO OF THE RISHI MOON

STATISTICS

SPECIES: Human
HEIGHT: 1.83 m (6 ft)
GENDER: Male
ALLEGIANCE: Republic
HOMEWORLD: Kamino
WEAPONS: Z-6 rotary cannon, DC-15 blaster pistol
TALENTS: Trained for combat, recon, and military tactics; handling heavy weapons
KNOWN COMPANIONS: Sergeant O'Niner, Fives, Echo

DOOM MISSION

The clones realize the only way to alert the Republic to the Separatist invasion of the Rishi Moon is to destroy their base. They wire the outpost to blow, but the detonator has to be triggered manually. Hevy volunteers, even though the mission is certain to be his last.

A COURTLY, EVEN FRIENDLY pirate, Hondo Ohnaka and his gang seize starships in the Outer Rim and ransom passengers. But he takes a big risk when he keeps the dangerous Count Dooku as a hostage.

Long pigtails are a pirate's pride

Goggles used for swoop-piloting

STATISTICS

SPECIES: Weequay
HEIGHT: 1.85 m (6 ft 1 in)
GENDER: Male
ALLEGIANCE: Neutral
HOMEWORLD: Sriluur
WEAPONS:
Vibroblade
TALENTS: Combat; leadership
KNOWN COMPANIONS:
Turk Falso, Gwarm, Aurra Sing, Pilf Mukmuk

Overcoat stolen from Wroonian

HONDO OHNAKA
SCOURGE OF THE SPACE LANES

Boots swiped from Corellian pirate

RANSOM RULES

Hondo Ohnaka likes a good fight as much as the next pirate, but he's tried to teach his gang a bit about pirate economics. Even when prisoners are rude, killing makes for bad business— dead men tell no tales, but they also bring in no credits for ransom.

THE LATEST IN A long line of battle droids, IG-86s are advertised as bodyguards or home defenders, but they are often used aggressively by underworld figures against their foes.

Vocoders and sound sensors

Rack of gas canisters

SHIP SECURITY

Gha Nachkt likes to let visitors to the *Vulture's Claw* pick through his salvage ship's hold full of junk, but the Trandoshan doesn't have time to babysit them. He's found a good answer to this dilemma: Several scavenged IG-86 droids keep their targeting sights on Gha's customers.

STATISTICS

SPECIES: Battle droid

HEIGHT: 1.99 m (6 ft 6 in)

GENDER: Male programming

ALLEGIANCE: Neutral

MANUFACTURER: Holowan Mechanicals

WEAPONS: Varies

EQUIPMENT: Variety of sensors

A YOUNG CORUSCANTI WOMAN, Ione Marcy seems to be witness to a murder. But Jedi investigator Tera Sinube can't help but wonder if the terrified Ione is really so scared—or so innocent. Trust an old investigator: In the absence of evidence, a story's just a story.

Underworld tattoos are current fashion

Cheap blouse bought at bazaar

Hand evolved from avian wing-claw

STATISTICS

SPECIES: Unknown
HEIGHT: 1.78 m (5 ft 10 in)
GENDER: Female
ALLEGIANCE: Neutral
HOMEWORLD: Coruscant
WEAPONS: None
TALENTS: Powerful friends
KNOWN COMPANIONS:
Cassie Cryar

IONE MARCY
WITNESS OR SUSPECT?

3:10 TO YAVIN

After escaping Tera Sinube and Ahsoka Tano, Ione and Cassie Cryar flee to Coruscant's network of rail stations, hoping to escape the authorities and make their way offworld. But the Jedi are close behind. Police droids grab Ione, but Cassie ignites Ahsoka's saber and starts swinging!

A LORD OF THE powerful Desilijic clan, Jabba controls strategic trade routes in the Outer Rim, and both the Republic and the Separatists seek a treaty with him. He dotes on Rotta, his young son, but is ruthless with his enemies, seeing all other beings only as sources of profit.

STATISTICS

SPECIES: Hutt
LENGTH: 3.9 m (12 ft 10 in)
GENDER: Male-dominant
ALLEGIANCE: Desilijic Kajidic
HOMEWORLD: Tatooine
WEAPONS: None
TALENTS: Running a criminal organization; fighting tough; leadership
KNOWN COMPANIONS: TC-70, Rotta the Huttlet, Ziro the Hutt

JABBA THE HUTT
INTERGALACTIC CRIME LORD

CRIMINAL WORMS

The Hutts have been kingpins of the galactic underworld for thousands of years, making credits from unsavory businesses like slaves, black-market spice, and smuggling. The Hutt clans constantly battle to outdo each other and take over each other's businesses, and Hutts view honesty and goodwill as signs of weakness that can be exploited.

Hutts see in the ultraviolet spectrum

Thick, muscular body lacks a skeleton

Powerful tail can be used as a club

NABOO'S ACCIDENT-PRONE representative to the Senate, Jar Jar seems to attract trouble and bad luck— for his enemies and his friends alike. He is exasperating, but also kind-hearted and loyal.

Gungans' haillu reveal emotions

Ceremonial Naboo decorations

STATISTICS

SPECIES: Gungan
HEIGHT: 1.96 m (6 ft 5 in)
GENDER: Male
ALLEGIANCE: Republic
HOMEWORLD: Naboo
WEAPONS: Clumsiness
TALENTS: Hard to describe
KNOWN COMPANIONS: Padmé Amidala, C-3PO, Captain Typho, Chancellor Palpatine

JAR JAR BINKS
GOOD-HEARTED GUNGAN

PLAGUE

The discovery of battle droids on Naboo means bad news for the planet: Her Separatist enemies have returned. But the mysterious death of Peppi Bow's shaaks suggests something worse: Plague is loose on the beautiful green world. Jar Jar and Padmé fear Separatist agents are seeking to poison the planet.

ADAPTABLE GUNGANS

Gungans adapt easily to any number of situations. They can live on land and in the water; speak Basic and their own language; and eat most anything their long tongues can snake out and catch.

Mottled skin offers excellent camouflage

A MECHANICAL GENIUS, YOUNG Jaybo Hood has made the best of his captivity on Iego, reprogramming Separatist battle droids to cater to his every whim. Jaybo thinks he can never leave the planet, so he figures he should at least live like a king.

Mind easily sees how droids work

JAYBO HOOD
KING OF THE DROIDS

Spare battery packs for machinery

ESCAPING IEGO

Jaybo believes that the Curse of Drol will keep Anakin and Obi-Wan stuck on Iego—after all, the ghosts have destroyed every other ship that tried to get away. But the Jedi's bravery and ability with the Force convince him to help them with their plan to escape.

Tunic made of cheap nerf hide

Reprogrammed droid caller

STATISTICS

SPECIES: Human
HEIGHT: 1.4 m (4 ft 7 in)
GENDER: Male
ALLEGIANCE: Neutral
HOMEWORLD: Iego
WEAPONS: None
TALENTS: Data-slicing; droid programming
KNOWN COMPANIONS: Amit Noloff, Anakin Skywalker, Obi-Wan Kenobi

FEW DUTIES ARE DULLER than being a heavy-weapons specialist in the Coruscant Guard. But Jek gets plenty of action when he's thrown into a wild battle on the coral moon of Rugosa: Asajj Ventress seems to have brought half the galaxy's clankers with her.

PLEX missile launcher

JEK
HAVE CHAINGUN WILL TRAVEL

STATISTICS

SPECIES: Human

HEIGHT: 1.83 m (6 ft)

GENDER: Male

ALLEGIANCE: Republic

HOMEWORLD: Kamino

WEAPONS: Z-6 rotary cannon, DC-15 blaster pistol, thermal detonator, PLEX missile launcher

TALENTS: Combat, recon, military tactics, and using heavy weapons

KNOWN COMPANIONS: Lieutenant Thire, Rys, Yoda

Beloved Z-6 rotary cannon

NEW IDEA

Jek has memorized the manual for every weapon in the clones' arsenal, and he's trained to use them on any battlefield. But on the coral moon, Yoda tries to teach Jek a new idea: The best weapon is the mind. It's flexible, and it will never run out of ammunition.

A FARMBOY ON SALEUCAMI, Jek has given little thought to the war dividing the galaxy. But all that changes when a mysterious stranger arrives on their farm—a stranger with the same face as Jek's father.

Surplus military helmet

Lekku reflect mixed parentage

JEK LAWQUANE
SON OF A MYSTERIOUS FATHER

STATISTICS

SPECIES: Human/Twi'lek
HEIGHT: 95 cm (3 ft 1 in)
GENDER: Male
ALLEGIANCE: Neutral
HOMEWORLD: Saleucami
WEAPONS: None
TALENTS: Farming
KNOWN COMPANIONS:
Suu Lawquane,
Shaeeh Lawquane,
Cut Lawquane,
Captain Rex

Jumpsuit stands up to play and chores

Drawing made for his father

ARRIVALS

Jek and his sister Shaeeah are happy at first to have someone new around the farm—sometimes it can be boring with no one to see but your sibling and your parents. But they get too much excitement when they accidentally activate a squad of General Grievous's deadly droids.

COMBAT HAS TAUGHT THE clone trooper Jester a valuable lesson: Take good care of your weapon and it will take good care of you. After every mission, self-disciplined Jester carefully cleans and maintains his blaster.

Carefully tended sideburns

Well-maintained DC-15 blaster

SAVED BY OLD HABITS

On Christophsis, Jester is nervous when Cody and Rex show up in his squad's barracks in search of a traitor: He'd much rather face a horde of clankers than superior officers asking questions. But Jester's alibi is ironclad: He was cleaning his gun when someone contacted the Separatists.

JESTER
HIS WEAPON IS HIS LIFE

Knee plate of plastoid armor

STATISTICS

SPECIES: Human

HEIGHT: 1.83 m (6 ft)

GENDER: Male

ALLEGIANCE: Republic

HOMEWORLD: Kamino

WEAPONS: Z-6 rotary cannon, DC-15 blaster pistol

TALENTS: Trained for combat, recon, military tactics, and handling heavy weapons

KNOWN COMPANIONS: Sergeant Slick, Chopper, Hawk, Punch, Gus, Sketch

CC-1993, OR "JET," SERVES under Jedi General Ki-Adi-Mundi, and is known for his distinctive, orange-hued armor. Jet's squads of flame troopers play a critical role in the fight to retake the Geonosis hives.

Experimental communications gear

Jet's unit is known for bold colors

JET
WARRIOR OF THE RED SANDS

STATISTICS

SPECIES: Human
HEIGHT: 1.83 m (6 ft)
GENDER: Male
ALLEGIANCE: Republic
HOMEWORLD: Kamino
WEAPONS: DC-15 blaster pistol
TALENTS: Combat, recon, and military tactics; heavy weapons handling
KNOWN COMPANIONS: Ki-Adi-Mundi, Captain Rex, Commander Cody

Kama treated to resist heat

TOUGH TASK

The briefing on Geonosis leaves Jet biting his lip beneath his helmet. This is going to be a tough fight, with Geonosians attacking from all directions. But that's the life of a soldier: The job's the job, no matter what the odds against you.

Twin Ansata hair sticks

Robes favored by Jedi historians

THE CHIEF LIBRARIAN OF THE Jedi Archives, Jocasta Nu is quite proud of the Order's accumulated knowledge—and impatient with talk that there are things about which the Jedi know little. To her, all that's worth knowing is already within the Jedi Archives.

JOCASTA NU
KEEPER OF THE JEDI ARCHIVES

SABER CLASH

Jocasta Nu can be impatient with Padawans, and a few have briefly thought how satisfying it would be to see if a lightsaber would make the old librarian more polite. Ahsoka Tano actually gets the chance—well, sort of—when she catches a bounty hunter masquerading as Jocasta.

STATISTICS

SPECIES: Human
HEIGHT: 1.69 m (5 ft 6 in)
GENDER: Female
ALLEGIANCE: Jedi Order
HOMEWORLD: Coruscant
WEAPONS: Lightsaber
TALENTS: Lightsaber combat; Force sensitivity; knowledge of the Jedi archives
KNOWN COMPANIONS: Yoda, Kit Fisto, Obi-Wan Kenobi, Ahsoka Tano, Tera Sinube, Mace Windu

A HIDDEN GEONOSIAN LEADER, KARINA the Great dwells in the catacombs beneath the Progate Temple, laying eggs and controlling an army of Geonosian drones that maintain her nest and defend her against all enemies.

KARINA THE GREAT
THE SECRET QUEEN

STATISTICS

SPECIES: Geonosian
HEIGHT: 8.6 m (28 ft 3 in)
GENDER: Female
ALLEGIANCE: Geonosian Hive
HOMEWORLD: Geonosis
WEAPONS: None
TALENTS: Dangerous in combat; commanding drone servants
KNOWN COMPANIONS: Poggle the Lesser

INVADERS!

At the beginning of the Clone Wars, the Republic's forces failed to discover that Poggle the Lesser took his orders from a mysterious queen. But now a desperate Poggle has led them to her lair beneath the ancient Progate Temple, where Karina the Great has secret defenses to surprise unwelcome invaders.

Crown of the Geonosian hive

Vestigial claws are of little practical use

Egg sac produces new hive drones

Three eyes offer superb vision

Ancient staff of mysterious origin

SECRET TRIP

Like most Gran, Kharrus is extremely loyal, and will do anything for the greater good of the Republic. The chance to capture Count Dooku and possibly end the war makes his trip to Florrum the most important mission of Kharrus's long career.

Clawed feet for digging up roots

KHARRUS
A GRAN ON A MISSION

STATISTICS

SPECIES: Gran
HEIGHT: 1.78 m (5 ft 10 in)
GENDER: Male
ALLEGIANCE: Republic
HOMEWORLD: Kinyen
WEAPONS: None
TALENTS: Diplomacy
KNOWN COMPANIONS: Jar Jar Binks, Chancellor Palpatine, Commander Stone

KI-ADI-MUNDI IS A RARITY among the Jedi: He is allowed to marry despite the Order's forbidding of emotional attachment. The birth rate on Cerea is so low that Cerean Jedi can have families, though Ki-Adi-Mundi rarely gets to see his.

Lightsaber held in Ataru stance

Second heart pumps blood to big brain

KI-ADI-MUNDI
CHAMPION OF CEREA

STATISTICS

SPECIES: Cerean

HEIGHT: 1.98 m (6 ft 6 in)

GENDER: Male

ALLEGIANCE: Jedi

HOMEWORLD: Cerea

WEAPONS: Lightsaber

TALENTS: Ataru lightsaber; combat; Force sensitivity; knowledge of military tactics; diplomacy

KNOWN COMPANIONS: Mace Windu, Yoda, Luminara Unduli, Obi-Wan Kenobi, Plo Koon

WELCOME BACK

Ki-Adi-Mundi was captured in the first Battle of Geonosis when his raid on a Droid Control Ship failed. He's determined that things will go better this time, and has spent hours looking over intelligence reports and discussing strategy with Commander Jet, looking for weaknesses in the defenses rebuilt by the Geonosians.

A PILOT IN THE fighter squadron attached to the Jedi Cruiser *Resolute*, Kickback flies as Blue Four in the devastating Battle of Ryloth, and is one of only two squadron members to survive. After the costly defeat, Kickback and Swoop must rebuild their squadron.

STATISTICS

SPECIES: Human

HEIGHT: 1.83 m (6 ft)

GENDER: Male

ALLEGIANCE: Republic

HOMEWORLD: Kamino

WEAPONS: DC-15 blaster pistol

TALENTS: Expert fighter pilot; military tactics

KNOWN COMPANIONS:

Ahsoka Tano, Axe, Swoop, Tucker

KICKBACK
RYLOTH SURVIVOR

HEAVY FIRE

Flying alongside Ahsoka in Blue Squadron, Kickback surveys the Separatist warships deployed around Ryloth and feels a twinge of unease. This isn't the usual unimaginative clanker defense: Someone with a sense of strategy is waiting for the Republic attack.

ADMIRAL KILIAN ISN'T A big man, but he projects an air of authority from decades in the Tynquay Sector Forces. He is a model officer, loyal to his ship, his crew, and the Republic.

KILIAN
YOUNG HUNTER'S HOSTAGE

Beard is kept carefully trimmed

Disc indicates officer status

Boots kept shined as per regulations

THIS SHIP IS HIS LIFE

The *Endurance* is Admiral Kilian's command, as well as his pride and joy. When an unknown saboteur damages her in space over Vanqor, Mace Windu and Anakin Skywalker urge the admiral to evacuate before it's too late, but the proud Kilian will do no such thing.

STATISTICS

SPECIES: Human
HEIGHT: 1.72 m (5 ft 8 in)
GENDER: Male
ALLEGIANCE: Republic
HOMEWORLD: Corellia
WEAPONS: DC-17 hand blaster
TALENTS: Leadership; extensive knowledge of military tactics; seasoned diplomat
KNOWN COMPANIONS: Anakin Skywalker, Mace Windu

Headdress of
Taris nobility

SENATOR FOR THE FADED city-world
of Taris, Kin Robb finds her planet
perilously close to the front lines.
Fearing attack, she aligns herself
with the peace movement of
Duchess Satine, hoping to ensure
the safety of her homeworld.

Rich gown for
Senatorial
affairs

STATISTICS

SPECIES: Human
HEIGHT: 2 m (6 ft 6 in)
GENDER: Female
ALLEGIANCE: Republic
HOMEWORLD: Taris
WEAPONS: None
TALENTS: Diplomacy;
knowledge of Republic law
KNOWN COMPANIONS: Duchess
Satine, Orn Free Taa,
Tal Merrik, Onaconda Farr

TESTED BY THE JEDI

Aboard the *Coronet*, Obi-Wan Kenobi
uses a captured assassin droid as a tool
to find out who has betrayed the ship to the
Separatists. The droid, he figures, will try
to attack everyone except the person who
programmed it. The spider-like droid
lunges at Kin Robb—she's innocent!

THE MONARCH OF THE Toydarians, Katuunko serves the Hutts—but still maintains his independence where he can. He arranges a meeting with the Republic on Rugosa's coral moon, but Asajj Ventress and her army are uninvited guests.

Toydarian knight's war helmet

Quick wing beats let Toydarians hover

KING KATUUNKO
WITNESS TO A WAGER

STATISTICS

SPECIES: Toydarian
HEIGHT: 1.52 m (5 ft)
GENDER: Male
ALLEGIANCE: Toydarians
HOMEWORLD: Toydaria
WEAPONS: Sword
TALENTS: Diplomacy

Ceremonial sword of royal office

HUTT SERVANTS

Toydarians sometimes keep secrets from their Hutt masters, like the existence of Rugosa's moon, with its swamps and warm seas. When the Hutts find out about the Toydarians' paradise, they release a plague that dries up its oceans.

Webbed feet for walking in mud

ABLE TO BREATHE AIR or water, Kit Fisto is known among the Jedi for his easygoing nature and ready smile. But he is also a fierce fighter, tireless in his efforts to combat the threat of the Separatists. Kit is compassionate, yet he knows the dangers of attachment for a Jedi.

Excellent vision even in low light

STATISTICS

SPECIES: Nautolan
HEIGHT: 1.96 m (6 ft 5 in)
GENDER: Male
ALLEGIANCE: Jedi Order
HOMEWORLD: Glee Anselm
WEAPONS: Lightsaber
TALENTS: Force-sensitivity; Shii-Cho lightsaber Master; acute senses; pheromone detection
KNOWN COMPANIONS: Nahdar Vebb, Aayla Secura, Plo Koon, R6-H5

KIT FISTO
A JEDI WITH A SMILE

Tentacles can sense others' pheromones

Kit sheds heavy boots to fight in water

TARGET: GRIEVOUS

Like his former Padawan Nahdar Vebb, Kit is excited to learn they've discovered the hideout of General Grievous. But Kit knows that the cyborg warlord is a clever, deadly enemy, even for Jedi who are strong in the Force. He and Nahdar must be cautious.

AN IG-86 SENTINEL droid, KRONOS-327 serves Ziro the Hutt as an assassin. The droid has eliminated many of Ziro's enemies, and the crime lord refuses to wipe his memory. But KRONOS's service counts for little after he fails Ziro on his latest mission.

KRONOS-327
ZIRO'S ASSASSIN

Cranium is packed with sensors

STATISTICS

SPECIES: IG-86 sentinel droid
HEIGHT: 1.99 m (6 ft 6 in)
GENDER: Male programming
ALLEGIANCE: Ziro the Hutt
MANUFACTURER: Holowan Mechanicals
WEAPONS: Underworld blaster rifle
FEATURES: Combat programming; knowledge of military tactics; sensor suite
KNOWN COMPANIONS: Ziro the Hutt

Superior ability to target enemies

Magnetic graspers grip weapons

Servos can move even in high gravity

TERMINATED

KRONOS-327 fails to kill one of Ziro's rivals on a mission to Yout 12, but is confident he can do so if given another chance. Unfortunately for KRONOS, Ziro doesn't believe in second chances. Before KRONOS can react, his weapons are deactivated and he's dragged away to be turned into spare parts.

KWAZEL MAWS STUN their prey by flashing their bioluminescent markings, then swallow them whole. They sometimes hunt for food in the lagoons of Rodia, finding the warmth to their liking—and sometimes doing lots of damage to the planet's domed cities while chasing prey.

Bioluminescent markings on skin

Giant mouth can swallow prey whole

Prolegs cling to walls of undersea canyons

STATISTICS

SPECIES: Kwazel maw
LENGTH: 88 m (288 ft 9 in)
HOMEWORLD: Rodia
WEAPONS: Stunning, fierce bite
ECOLOGY: Kwazel maws dwell in the seas of Rodia, where they are among the top predators

KWAZEL MAW
LORD OF THE RODIAN DEPTHS

RUINED PLANS

Nute Gunray thinks he has his revenge at last: Padmé Amidala is captured, and his droids will soon find the missing Gungan Jedi. But Gunray hasn't counted on the arrival of an angry kwazel maw for whom battle droids were just bite-sized morsels.

Thick tail allows speedy swimming

THESE DIMINUTIVE SERVANT droids were originally built for childcare, but have proved useful as valets and assistants, able to perform tasks from serving tea to hiding virus-laden explosives. One LEP is hiding in Dr. Vindi's lab—and carries the potential to ruin Naboo.

LEP SERVANT DROID
TEA? VIRUS BOMB?

Antennas carry transmissions

Cute features appeal to children

FOLLOWING ORDERS

LEP-86C8 seems an unlikely agent for the destruction of all life in the galaxy, but that's what could happen if the little droid's bomb explodes and infects Naboo's atmosphere. Jar Jar, Padmé, and a squad of clones hunt LEP-86C8 in a dangerous game of hide-and-seek.

Delicate fingers can grasp small objects

STATISTICS

SPECIES: Service droid
HEIGHT: 1.26 m (4 ft 2 in)
GENDER: Various programming
ALLEGIANCE: Neutral
MANUFACTURER: Coachelle Automata
WEAPONS: None
EQUIPMENT: Storage compartment

Round stomach is used for storage

A HEAVYSET NEIMOIDIAN weapons maker, Lok Durd dreams that his creations will turn the tide of the war and bring him the glory he deserves. He selects Maridun as the place to test his latest dreadful weapon, the Defoliator.

Neimoidian mitre denotes high status

Face swollen from huge appetites

LOK DURD
IMMORAL INVENTOR

STATISTICS

SPECIES: Neimoidian
HEIGHT: 2.11 m (6 ft 11 in)
GENDER: Male
ALLEGIANCE: Separatists
HOMEWORLD: Neimoidia
WEAPONS: None
TALENTS: Weapons research; ruthless leadership
KNOWN COMPANIONS: Count Dooku

FIELD TEST

The weapon codenamed the Defoliator is designed to burn away living matter without harming the droids of the Separatists' armies. On Maridun, Durd selects two hapless battle droids as subjects for a test of the new weapon.

LOLO PURS ASSISTS SENATOR Onaconda Farr with defending Rodia's interests on Coruscant. She feels betrayed by the fact that Farr briefly worked with the Separatists in order to protect their planet.

Expression is determined

Hold-out pistol is small but deadly

LOLO PURS
RODIAN REPRESENTATIVE

REVENGE

Lolo Purs has tried to forgive Ono for his treachery: If Padmé can give her old friend another chance, why can't she do the same? But she finds it impossible to get over her anger and shame, and decides the Senator must pay with his life.

Yellow sash worn in spring on Rodia

STATISTICS

SPECIES: Rodian
HEIGHT: 1.75 m (5 ft 9 in)
GENDER: Female
ALLEGIANCE: Republic
HOMEWORLD: Rodia
WEAPONS: Hold-out deactivator pistol
TALENTS: Knowledge of legislative strategy
KNOWN COMPANIONS: Onaconda Farr, Silood, Mon Mothma, Padmé Amidala, Bail Organa

THE TRADE FEDERATION'S representative, Lott Dod remains in the Senate at the request of those in the Republic who push for peace. As a Senator, he pursues Count Dooku's agenda all but openly —when he's not meeting Separatist leaders on Cato Neimoidia.

Miter indicates
Senatorial rank

Scowl seems to
be permanent

WEAKNESS IS ONLY HUMAN

Lott Dod is surprised when Scipio's Rush Clovis brings Padmé Amidala, one of the Trade Federation's sworn enemies, to Cato Neimoidia. But Clovis's infatuation with the beautiful Padmé gives Dod an idea: By poisoning her, he can gain a better deal from Clovis and his Banking Clan. How like a human to be led around by his emotions!

LOTT DOD
FACE OF THE FEDERATION

STATISTICS

SPECIES: Neimoidian
HEIGHT: 1.9 m (6 ft 3 in)
GENDER: Male
ALLEGIANCE: Separatists
HOMEWORLD: Cato Neimoidia
WEAPONS: None
KNOWN COMPANIONS: Rush Clovis, Poggle the Lesser

Mantle reflects
high Neimoidian
status

A BY-THE-BOOK JEDI KNOWN as a tough, tradition-minded taskmaster, Luminara Unduli thinks Jedi should be respectful, not reckless. She has worked to make her own Padawan, Barriss Offee, into a model apprentice.

LUMINARA UNDULI
OLD-SCHOOL JEDI

Emerald-bladed lightsaber

Tattoo denoting Mirial adept status

STATISTICS

SPECIES: Mirialan
HEIGHT: 1.7 m (5 ft 7 in)
GENDER: Female
ALLEGIANCE: Jedi Order
HOMEWORLD: Mirial
WEAPONS: Lightsaber
TALENTS: Force-sensitivity; mind-probing; diplomacy
KNOWN COMPANIONS: Barriss Offee, Ahsoka Tano, Anakin Skywalker, Obi-Wan Kenobi

DARK DUEL

Luminara's strict discipline makes it hard for her to believe that a wild, untrained user of the Force like Asajj Ventress could ever be her equal in lightsaber combat. Aboard the *Tranquility*, she discovers her error: Ventress's rage gives her surprising power.

Mirial sash made of heveng wool

A GRIM JEDI MASTER, Mace Windu is famous for his skills with his lightsaber, with its instantly recognizable amethyst blade. He is suspicious of the Galactic Senate and is determined to undo the Separatists' plots and destroy them.

Well-known saber with amethyst blade

Traditional robes of a Jedi warrior

MACE WINDU
KEEPER OF THE JEDI FLAME

STATISTICS

SPECIES: Human
HEIGHT: 1.88 m (6 ft 2 in)
GENDER: Male
ALLEGIANCE: Jedi Order
HOMEWORLD: Haruun Kal
WEAPONS: Lightsaber
TALENTS: Force-sensitivity; Vaapad lightsaber style; shatterpoint ability; diplomacy; leadership
KNOWN COMPANIONS: Yoda, Obi-Wan Kenobi, Anakin Skywalker, Commander Ponds, Razor, Stak, Cham Syndulla

SABERS UP

Mace Windu is a patient diplomat when he needs to be, and avoids the use of force if he can. But he knows that the Separatist threat can't be defeated by politicians—only Jedi and their clone troops will end this war. When the talking ends, he ignites his saber with a stoic determination.

IG-100 DROIDS SERVE as bodyguards for top Separatist leaders. These deadly droids are fast, tough, and can keep fighting even after their heads are cut off. Battling them is a tough task even for an experienced Jedi Knight.

MAGNAGUARD
WALKING DOOM

STATISTICS

SPECIES: Battle droid
HEIGHT: 1.95 m (6 ft 5 in)
GENDER: Male programming
ALLEGIANCE: Separatists
MANUFACTURER: Holowan Mechanicals
WEAPONS: Electrostaff
EQUIPMENT: Magnetic feet, sensors

Photoreceptors glow angry red

Armor plate guards connectors

Electropole can stun or kill

Heavy feet are surprisingly nimble

NEVER A FAIR FIGHT

MagnaGuards are programmed to fight in groups, spinning their electrostaffs in deadly circles and ganging up on their enemies until they make a fatal mistake. Sadly, many a Jedi has made such an error.

IT ISN'T EASY being the mother of a Force-sensitive child—Mahtee knows that one day the Jedi will arrive to take her son Wee away to Coruscant. But until then she will do anything it takes to protect him, as any mother would.

FUTURE JEDI

Mahtee realizes very early that Wee is no ordinary Rodian baby: He's able to levitate toys almost from the day of his birth. She enjoys watching her son practice his skills, and dreams that one day he will be a great Jedi.

Easy-to-clean vest is good for spit-ups

Tiny suction-cup fingertips

Wee Dunn likes these shiny plates

MAHTEE DUNN
RODIAN MOTHER

DECEIT REVEALED

Disguised as a Jedi, Cad Bane warns Mahtee that fake Jedi are stealing children. She pulls a gun on Obi-Wan when he arrives on the hunter's trail, and is horrified to learn she was tricked into handing over Wee.

STATISTICS

SPECIES: Rodian
HEIGHT: 1.7 m (5 ft 7 in)
GENDER: Female
ALLEGIANCE: Neutral
HOMEWORLD: Rodia
WEAPONS: LL-30 blaster pistol
TALENTS: Maternal instinct
KNOWN COMPANIONS: Wee Dunn

THE MANDALORIAN ROYAL GUARD PROTECT Duchess Satine. She is a pacifist, but she knows that she has enemies among those who won't give up the old ways. Her guards are a formidable force, but are trained to show restraint.

Helmet used for ceremonial events

Gorget is remnant of full body armor

Electrostaff can paralyze opponent

MANDALORIAN ROYAL GUARD
SATINE'S DEFENDERS

STATISTICS

SPECIES: Human

HEIGHT: Varies

GENDER: Male

ALLEGIANCE: Mandalore

HOMEWORLD: Mandalore

WEAPONS: Electrostaff

EQUIPMENT:
Communications gear

THE NEW TRADITION

The crisp uniforms and proud helms worn by the Mandalorian Guard are meant to evoke the planet's traditions of gallantry and discipline while rejecting the violent past of its warrior clans.

STATISTICS

SPECIES: Human

HEIGHT: Varies

GENDER: Male

ALLEGIANCE: Death Watch

HOMEWORLD: Mandalore

WEAPONS: Various blasters

EQUIPMENT: Armor, jetpack

MANDALORE'S NOMADS WERE ONCE FEARED throughout the galaxy. These days their warrior clans are believed to be just memories, having been defeated by the Jedi long ago. But as Duchess Satine discovers, their threat remains.

Helmet design is ancient tradition

Jetpack topped with explosive missile

LUNAR SECRET

Mandalore's officials insist that Jango Fett was nothing more than a bounty hunter in scrounged armor and that their planet's warriors were exiled to Concordia and died out long ago. But on Mandalore's moon, Obi-Wan Kenobi finds that isn't true.

Gauntlets mount various weapons

Tactical boots with magnetic soles

MANDALORIAN WARRIOR
DEVOTEE OF THE DEATH WATCH

THE VETERAN NAVAL OFFICER Mar Tuuk leads the Separatist blockade of Ryloth. He respects Anakin Skywalker, his Republic opponent, but has no doubt that he can out-think the young Jedi. However, Tuuk discovers that some Jedi are less predictable than he imagined.

Sensor goggles link to ship systems

A good officer leads with his chin

MAR TUUK
SEPARATIST STRATEGIST

STATISTICS

SPECIES: Neimoidian

HEIGHT: 2.09 m (6 ft 10 in)

GENDER: Male

ALLEGIANCE: Separatists

HOMEWORLD: Neimoidia

WEAPONS: Blaster pistol

TALENTS: Military tactics; leadership; evasion

Fingers knit in contemplation

IRRATIONAL JEDI

After turning back the first attack on his blockade, Mar Tuuk predicts that Anakin Skywalker will be back with his forces for another try. And he's correct. But nothing could have led Tuuk to guess that Anakin would try something as crazy as flying a shattered Jedi Cruiser all by himself—or guiding the ruined warship onto a collision course with Mar Tuuk's Neimoidian flagship.

THE VICE CHAIRMAN OF the Galactic Senate, Mas Amedda presides over the chamber during debates and works behind the scenes to ensure that the programs of Chancellor Palpatine will be adopted, using all his political skills to do so.

Speaker's staff topped with statue

Lethorns thicken as Chagrians age

Chagrians wear red during times of war

STATISTICS

SPECIES: Chagrian
HEIGHT: 1.96 m (6 ft 5 in)
GENDER: Male
ALLEGIANCE: Republic
HOMEWORLD: Chagria
WEAPONS: None
TALENTS: Bureaucracy;
   diplomacy; playing the
   politics game
KNOWN COMPANIONS:
   Orn Free Taa,
   Chancellor Palpatine

MAS AMEDDA
SENATE POWER BROKER

CRISIS AT MANDALORE

After a recording comes to light of Mandalore's Deputy Minister Jerec warning that the Death Watch cult threatens the planet, Amedda moves swiftly to line up support for a Republic military intervention.

DESCENDED FROM FLYING creatures, mastiff phalones have traded wings for powerful clawed limbs. These ferocious predators prefer to hunt by night, but will track vulnerable prey in daylight as well and they fear nothing on their planet.

MASTIFF PHALONE
TERRORS OF MARIDUN

STATISTICS

SPECIES: Mastiff phalone
HEIGHT: 2 m (6 ft 6 in)
HOMEWORLD: Maridun
WEAPONS: Fierce bite, stabbing claws
ECOLOGY: Mastiff phalones prowl Maridun's plains in packs, and are the savage planet's top predators

FROM THE DARK

Captain Rex's helmet includes audio pickups that give him superb hearing and infrared vision. But he is busy treating Anakin Skywalker's injuries, and mastiff phalones move with such speed and stealth that Rex never hears them until they've begun their attack.

Males use feathers in courtship displays

Teeth hold prey during attacks

Razor-sharp claws deliver killing slashes

Wings evolved back into powerful limbs

- Republic logo on flight helmet

- Life-support system and monitors

- Special body glove for high gravity

A TOUGH, CONFIDENT CLONE trooper pilot, Matchstick welcomes the chance to fly a new Y-wing into battle against Grievous's *Malevolence*, despite suffering damage on the way to the fight. A pilot trusts his own abilities —and those of his squadmates.

DRIVER'S SEAT

Pilots need exceptional eyesight, extremely fast reflexes, and the ability to track what's happening on all sides of them while moving at high speeds. Kaminoan trainers test clones very early to discover which trainees are best-suited for duty behind the stick of a shuttle, gunship, bomber, or starfighter.

MATCHSTICK
SHADOW SQUADRON ACE

STATISTICS

SPECIES: Human

HEIGHT: 1.83 m (6 ft)

GENDER: Male

ALLEGIANCE: Republic

HOMEWORLD: Kamino

WEAPONS: DC-15 blaster pistol

TALENTS: Expert fighter pilot; military tactics

KNOWN COMPANIONS: Anakin Skywalker, Broadside, Ahsoka Tano, Plo Koon

MEDCHA WANTO
TALZ SCRIBE

AS SCRIBE TO THI-SEN, Medcha Wanto often speaks for Orto Plutonia's Talz tribe. His communication talents are tested by the arrival of strange, hairless bipeds from outer space. But to Medcha's happy surprise, the odd new arrivals prove much smarter than they look.

Headdress of animal hide

STATISTICS

SPECIES: Talz
HEIGHT: 2.48 m (8 ft 2 in)
GENDER: Male
ALLEGIANCE: Talz
HOMEWORLD: Orto Plutonia
WEAPONS: Spear
TALENTS: Diplomacy; knowledge of clan traditions; narglatch riding; combat
KNOWN COMPANIONS: Thi-Sen

Larger eyes shut in bright conditions

Crude drawing of battle droid

IN THE ICE

The Talz have dwelled on Orto Plutonia for eons, wishing only to be left alone in their icy villages. They pass down the stories of the great clans and the taming of the narglatches. But now, new stories must be written—tales of a war with sky-dwellers who would not let the Talz live their lives in peace.

THE VETERAN SENATOR FROM the Core World of Chandrila, Mon Mothma is respected at the highest levels of the Republic. She is a mentor to Padmé and a measured friend to the sometimes reckless Senator Bail Organa.

STATISTICS

SPECIES: Human
HEIGHT: 1.83 m (6 ft)
GENDER: Female
ALLEGIANCE: Republic
HOMEWORLD: Chandrila
WEAPONS: None
TALENTS: Diplomacy; organizational abilities; leadership
KNOWN COMPANIONS: Padmé Amidala, Bail Organa, Onaconda Farr, Chancellor Palpatine

Welcoming expression

Hanna pendant from Chandrila

Robes made of shimmersilk

MON MOTHMA
A VOICE OF CAUTION

SENATE INTRIGUE

Convinced no military solution can end the war, Mon Mothma and her Senate allies work to craft a bill to cut military spending and the production of more clone troops on Kamino. But their efforts are sharply opposed by Kaminoan Senator Halle Burtoni and the political bloc she's assembled.

THE NABOO ROYAL GUARD DEFEND the planet's monarch in Theed and during offworld missions. They are alert for trouble on the lush green world, searching for signs of Separatist spies who may have returned to cause further trouble.

Combat helmet with chin strap

Lightweight armor built for speed

NABOO ROYAL GUARD
WARDENS OF THEED

STATISTICS

SPECIES: Human

HEIGHT: Varies

GENDER: Varies

ALLEGIANCE: Naboo

HOMEWORLD: Naboo

WEAPONS: S-5 blaster pistol

EQUIPMENT: Helmets, communications gear, padded armor

Utility belt with ammo pouches

DEADLY RETURN

It's been years since battle droids were seen on Naboo, but a patrol ambushes a flight of STAPs escorting a tactical droid. In Theed, the droid reveals there's a secret Separatist lab somewhere in the Naboo swamps.

Shin protectors over short boots

A YOUNG JEDI KNIGHT, NAHDAR Vebb is Kit Fisto's former Padawan. Vebb loves his old Master, but he has grown impatient with the Jedi Order. He believes the war calls for speed and strength, not the caution and patience preached by wiser Jedi.

GRIEVOUS MUST PAY

As Nahdar explores Grievous's lair with Kit Fisto, the young Jedi feels his anger grow. Grievous has killed many Jedi, taking their lightsabers as trophies. But no more, Nahdar thinks—he will put an end to this evil.

STATISTICS

SPECIES: Mon Calamari
HEIGHT: 1.86 m (6 ft 1 in)
GENDER: Male
ALLEGIANCE: Jedi Order
HOMEWORLD: Mon Calamari
WEAPONS: Lightsaber
TALENTS: Force-sensitivity; lightsaber combat
KNOWN COMPANIONS: Kit Fisto, Fil

NAHDAR VEBB
PASSIONATE FORMER PADAWAN

Traditional Jedi robes made of rough cloth

Webbed hands for superb swimming

Lightsaber of a new Jedi Knight

TO MOST KAMINOANS, the Republic's clone troopers are little more than a successful product. But Nala Se is different. She cares deeply about each one, seeking to heal those injured in battle and staying with them even when her own life is threatened by a Separatist assault.

Long neck with limited flexibility

NALA SE
CLONE CARETAKER

STATISTICS

SPECIES: Kaminoan
HEIGHT: 2.13 m (7 ft)
GENDER: Female
ALLEGIANCE: Kaminoans
HOMEWORLD: Kamino
WEAPONS: None
TALENTS: Mastery of cloning techniques; medical care

Tubing to serum sample pouches

SPACE HOSPITAL

The secret Kaliida Shoals medical center, located near Naboo, takes in clone troops injured in battles across the Outer Rim. There, Nala Se supervises the care of more than 60,000 injured troops, all of them desperately needed on new battlefronts. But grim news reaches the station: Its secret has been discovered and General Grievous's battleship is on its way.

Boots built for slender Kaminoan feet

STATISTICS

SPECIES: Narglatch
HEIGHT: 6.2 m (20 ft 4 in)
HOMEWORLD: Orto Plutonia, Naboo, and others
WEAPONS: Bite
ECOLOGY: Narglatches are strong, fast hunters who are found on a number of different worlds

ORTO PLUTONIA'S NARGLATCHES are regarded as near-sacred by the Talz, who ride the great cats into battle and use their bones, meat, and hides for food, shelter, and offerings to the spirits of the ice. Without these mighty beasts, the Talz would barely survive themselves.

NARGLATCH
STEALTHY SNOW CAT

SHOWDOWN

After efforts to make peace with the Pantorans fail, Thi-Sen's warriors ride their narglatches into battle. The great cats may not be as fast as clone troopers' Freeco bikes, but their claws dig into the snow and ice, making quick turns, and their claws and teeth are as deadly at close quarters as a blaster or a spear.

Fleshy spikes end in sharp quills

Older males have longer chin quills

Saddle crafted from narglatch hide

Tail is held straight for better balance

NUMA HIDES FROM SEPARATISTS IN the ruins of Nabat until she is found by Boil and Waxer. She leads them to safety and teaches them about how humanity can be lost in war—but also saved.

NUMA
RYLOTH REFUGEE

STATISTICS

SPECIES: Twi'lek
HEIGHT: 1 m (3 ft 3 in)
GENDER: Female
ALLEGIANCE: Neutral
HOMEWORLD: Ryloth
WEAPONS: None
TALENTS: Knows secret ways through Nabat; bravery
KNOWN COMPANIONS: Boil, Waxer

Traditional Twi'lek headdress

The stress of war has numbed Numa

Dirty dress is her only remaining garment

Tooka doll escapes the ruin of Numa's home

FREEDOM FOR NABAT

Numa leads the clone troopers Boil and Waxer through the tunnels beneath Nabat—secret routes that bypass the Separatist defenses. After a short battle, Nabat is free, and Numa is reunited with her uncle.

MORE DROIDS?

Numa is terrified when she sees two tall figures in gleaming white, with skull-like heads. Surely these are more droids like the ones that destroyed her home? But to Numa's surprise, beneath their helmets the new arrivals are flesh and blood like her.

NUTE GUNRAY IS THE VICEROY of the Trade Federation. His dispute years ago with the Republic led to the Clone Wars. He hates Padmé Amidala and burns to avenge his humiliation at her hands by arranging her death. But his obsession may be his undoing.

Rich Neimoidian headdress

Permanent scowl causes wrinkles

PLOT FOILED!

After his plot to capture Padmé fails on Rodia, Nute Gunray is taken prisoner aboard a Jedi Cruiser. Next stop: Coruscant and a prison cell. Gunray's only hope is that Count Dooku values him too much to let him remain captive. But will Dooku's agents arrive in time to save him?

NUTE GUNRAY
VINDICTIVE VICEROY

Vibrant robes of Ramordian silk

STATISTICS

SPECIES: Neimoidian
HEIGHT: 1.91 m (6 ft 3 in)
GENDER: Male
ALLEGIANCE: Separatists
HOMEWORLD: Neimoidia
WEAPONS: None
TALENTS: Deal-making; political influence
KNOWN COMPANIONS: Asajj Ventress, General Grievous, Count Dooku

NUVO VINDI IS A BRILLIANT researcher, but also a madman. Working secretly for the Separatists, he has recreated the deadly Blue Shadow Virus, which he now hopes to unleash, destroying all other life in the galaxy.

Spectacles of Permese glass

NUVO VINDI
MAD SCIENTIST

STATISTICS

SPECIES: Faust
HEIGHT: 2.07 m
(6 ft 10 in)
GENDER: Male
ALLEGIANCE: Separatists
HOMEWORLD: Adana
WEAPONS: None
TALENTS: Scientific knowledge; genetic engineering

Lab researcher's overcoat

Health monitor affixed to arm

FATHER OF PLAGUES

Dr. Vindi's years of work in his underground lab have finally paid off: He's perfected variants of the Blue Shadow Virus that spread through the water and through the air. Jedi and clone troopers invade his lab, but Vindi isn't worried: His bombs will spread the virus to Naboo's surface and the rest of the galaxy.

Airtight boots for laboratory work

CT 19-7409, OR "SERGEANT O'NINER," is assigned to the Rishi Moon, where he works to keep his squad of bored rookies ready for combat. It's quiet on the Rim, but O'Niner knows that quiet times don't last.

Brow furrowed by stress of war

Helmet is dirty from many battles

Plastoid armor is pitted by minor damage

STATISTICS

SPECIES: Human
HEIGHT: 1.83 m (6 ft)
GENDER: Male
ALLEGIANCE: Republic
HOMEWORLD: Kamino
WEAPONS: DC-15 blaster pistol
TALENTS: Combat, recon, and military tactics; leadership
KNOWN COMPANIONS: Hevy, Fives, Echo

O'NINER
WATCHER ON THE RIM

FATAL DUTY

O'Niner has seen action in battles such as on Geonosis and the Celestial Wake, and he knows the attack by battle droids on the Rishi Moon outpost means a major invasion is coming. He tries to warn Republic forces, but is cut down by blaster fire before he can send a message to any nearby military units.

ANAKIN SKYWALKER'S FORMER Master, Obi-Wan Kenobi is a superb swordsman and expert negotiator. While deadly in battle, he has no love of war, and stubbornly seeks peaceful solutions in every conflict.

OBI-WAN KENOBI
JEDI NEGOTIATOR

Lightsaber held in Soresu stance

Forearm armor prevents nicks and cuts

ANAKIN'S MENTOR

Anakin Skywalker is now a Jedi Knight with a Padawan of his own. But Obi-Wan still worries about his former apprentice, and tries to help him escape his emotional attachments without losing his compassion.

Utility pouches hold odds and ends

DIPLOMACY

Obi-Wan's ability to ease volatile situations makes him one of the Republic's more valuable negotiators, and an obvious choice for missions that call for the prestige of a Jedi Knight. Such missions have sent Obi-Wan to meet the likes of Jabba the Hutt and Duchess Satine.

STATISTICS

SPECIES: Human
HEIGHT: 1.79 m (5 ft 10 in)
GENDER: Male
ALLEGIANCE: Jedi Order
HOMEWORLD: Coruscant
WEAPONS: Lightsaber
TALENTS: Ataru and Soresu lightsaber combat; Force sensitivity; negotiating; leadership
KNOWN COMPANIONS: Anakin Skywalker, Yoda, Mace Windu, Ahsoka Tano, Commander Cody

THESE TERRIFYING COMBAT droids rake their enemies with fire from a trio of laser cannons and can be modified to spray virus-laden gases. Even-larger models are known to have been built for use in the fearsome Separatist arsenal.

RUIN ON THE RIM

Determined to take Christophsis, the Separatists assemble a mighty force: Battle droids, super battle droids, retail droids, and droidekas, backed up by AAT tanks and heavy artillery. But the scariest sight of all is the giant virus octuptarra combat droids marching slowly but steadily on their trio of spindly legs.

STATISTICS

SPECIES: Battle droid
HEIGHT: 3.6 m (11 ft 10 in)
GENDER: None programmed
ALLEGIANCE: Separatists
MANUFACTURER: Techno Union
WEAPONS: Laser cannons
EQUIPMENT: Virus emitters

Cognitive module and sensor suite

Each laser cannon has optical sensor

Triple-jointed hydraulic limbs

OCTUPTARRA COMBAT DROID
DEATH FROM ABOVE

JEDI BUSINESS

Even veteran clone troopers pause before attacking an octuptarra droid. But Anakin Skywalker shows neither fear nor hesitation, meeting the giant droids with his lightsaber blazing.

ODDBALL IS AN EXPERT PILOT who's flown alongside Obi-Wan Kenobi on many missions. At the Battle of Teth, he once again learns to rely on his wingman, and to keep his cool behind the stick. A single pilot doesn't stand a chance, but a squadron can beat the odds.

Symbol of the Republic

Plastoid hose delivers air

ODDBALL
JEDI WINGMAN

STATISTICS

SPECIES: Human

HEIGHT: 1.83 m (6 ft)

GENDER: Male

ALLEGIANCE: Republic

HOMEWORLD: Kamino

WEAPONS: DC-15 blaster pistol

TALENTS: Expert fighter pilot; military tactics

KNOWN COMPANIONS: Obi-Wan Kenobi, Commander Cody

A CLOSE CALL

At Teth, Oddball and his fellow pilots are sent to rescue Anakin, Ahsoka, and Captain Rex from the B'omarr monastery. In the furious fight, a vulture droid scores a hit on Oddball's fighter. To his embarrassment, he panics—and needs Obi-Wan Kenobi to make a quick rescue.

RODIAN SENATOR ONACONDA FARR IS an old friend of Padmé Amidala's, having worked closely with her father helping the galaxy's refugees. But when Rodia faces starvation, Farr agrees to hand Padmé over to Nute Gunray in exchange for desperately needed relief.

Eyes can see in infrared spectrum

ONACONDA FARR
A QUESTION OF LOYALTY

HARD CHOICES

The Outer Rim world of Rodia has the bad luck to be caught between Republic and Separatist forces. Without a steady flow of trade ships, its people soon need food and medicine. Nute Gunray seeks to take advantage of the planet's woes and plans a trap for his old enemy Padmé Amidala.

Formal gown for Senate business

STATISTICS

SPECIES: Rodian
HEIGHT: 1.75 m (5 ft 9 in)
GENDER: Male
ALLEGIANCE: Republic
HOMEWORLD: Rodia
WEAPONS: None
TALENTS: Diplomacy; making deals; legislative strategy
KNOWN COMPANIONS: Silood, Lolo Purs, Padmé Amidala, Mon Mothma, Bail Organa

ORD ENISENCE IS one of many Jedi killed far from Coruscant in the fight against Count Dooku's Separatists. After his death, he plays a role in Cad Bane's plan to sneak into the Jedi Temple on Coruscant when the shapeshifter Cato Parasitti mimics his form and identity.

Newborns use ridge to break out of egg

ORD ENISENCE
MORE THAN MEETS THE EYE

STATISTICS

SPECIES: Skrilling
HEIGHT: 1.83 m (6 ft)
GENDER: Male
ALLEGIANCE: Jedi Order
HOMEWORLD: Agriworld-2079
WEAPONS: Lightsaber
TALENTS: Force-sensitivity; lightsaber combat

Powerful fingers offer crushing grip

RECLUSIVE SCHOLAR

Eager to demonstrate that she's learned from her mistakes on Felucia, Ahsoka Tano rushes to help Ord Enisence in the Jedi Library. But the gruff old Jedi just barks at Ahsoka to leave him in peace. Some days you can't do anything right.

A CORPULENT, CORRUPT Twi'lek Senator from Ryloth, Orn Free Taa is an example of all that is rotten with the Republic. His connections and political power make him a key ally of Chancellor Palpatine, though Twi'leks such as Cham Syndulla regard him as an enemy of progress.

STATISTICS

SPECIES: Twi'lek
HEIGHT: 1.84 m (6 ft)
GENDER: Male
ALLEGIANCE: Republic
HOMEWORLD: Ryloth
WEAPONS: None
TALENTS: Diplomacy; politics; leadership
KNOWN COMPANIONS: Chancellor Palpatine, Mas Amedda, Kin Robb, Tal Merrik

Jowls are evidence of vast appetites

Gaudy robe made of Ottegan silk

ORN FREE TAA
GREEDY POLITICIAN

CHECK PLEASE

Dinner on Duchess Satine's luxurious ship the *Coronet* is enough to satisfy the appetites of even the massive Orn Free Taa. He isn't hungry when Obi-Wan presents the Senators with a less than appealing dessert: Assassin Droid Under Glass.

PADMÉ AMIDALA WORKS FOR peace as the Senator from Naboo. She is secretly married to Anakin Skywalker and dreams of a quiet life with her beloved, far from war. But the call of duty is too strong.

Rank badge indicating Senatorial status

PADMÉ AMIDALA
SENATOR WITH A SECRET

TAKING AIM

Padmé likes to look for the good in people, but she isn't naïve, having seen firsthand what a Separatist occupation did to her homeworld of Naboo. Padmé isn't exactly a damsel in distress: When given no other choice she can hold her own with a blaster, and has had extensive experience at what she likes to call "aggressive negotiations."

Jumpsuit worn for space travel

STATISTICS

SPECIES: Human

HEIGHT: 1.65 m (5 ft 5 in)

GENDER: Female

ALLEGIANCE: Republic

HOMEWORLD: Naboo

WEAPONS: ELG-3A blaster pistol

TALENTS: Diplomacy

KNOWN COMPANIONS: Anakin Skywalker, C-3PO, Jar Jar Binks, Bail Organa, Onaconda Farr

Reinforced boots for travel

THE PANTORAN GUARD SERVES the Pantoran Assembly, which is led by the fanatic Chairman Chi Cho. On Orto Plutonia they defend Cho in his doomed offensive against the Talz, protecting the chairman until he collapses, mortally wounded by a Talz spear.

Beret bears symbol of Pantoran Guard

Livery of Pantoran Assembly

Ceremonial blaster rifle in sheath

STATISTICS

SPECIES: Pantoran
HEIGHT: Varies
GENDER: Male
ALLEGIANCE: Pantora
HOMEWORLD: Pantora
WEAPONS: DC-15 blaster pistol, ceremonial blaster rifle
EQUIPMENT: Ceremonial uniforms, communications gear

BATTLE IN THE ICE

The members of the Pantoran Guard are hand-picked by Chairman Chi Cho for their unquestioning loyalty as well as for their bravery and skill. The Guardsmen fight against the Talz without complaint, even though they know their defensive position is poor. To do otherwise would be to betray their oath to Pantora.

A GUNGAN HERDER, Peppi Bow wants only to care for the shaaks that rely on her. But when something in the water kills her animals, Peppi knows it's time to sound the alarm in Theed.

PEPPI BOW
HUMBLE HERDER

Flexible
Gungan neck

Colorful top of
Gungan weave

Trousers dyed
with pom-berry
extract

STATISTICS

SPECIES: Gungan

HEIGHT: 2.01 m (6 ft 7 in)

GENDER: Female

ALLEGIANCE: Neutral

HOMEWORLD: Naboo

WEAPONS: Electropole

TALENTS: Shaak husbandry; knowledge of Naboo flora and fauna; agility

KNOWN COMPANIONS:
A bunch of shaaks

Electropole used
to herd shaaks

ON THE HUNT

Peppi Bow knows nothing of war, but she's determined to find out what killed her shaaks, even if it means a trip into the dangerous Eastern Swamps. After Padmé and Jar Jar fail to return from their search, Peppi leads Ahsoka Tano up the river in search of the source of the disease in the water.

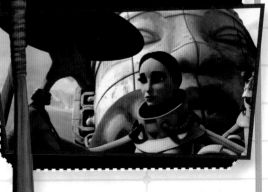

A RED-SKINNED KOWAKIAN monkey-lizard, Pilf Mukmuk is Hondo Ohnaka's beloved mascot, who ranges freely around the pirate base on Florrum getting into mischief. He has a yellow-skinned brother named Pikk, who is also expert at spying and sneaking.

STATISTICS

SPECIES: Kowakian monkey-lizard
HEIGHT: 58 cm (1 ft 11 in)
GENDER: Male
ALLEGIANCE: Hondo Ohnaka's gang
HOMEWORLD: Florrum
WEAPONS: None
TALENTS: Stealing; sneaking; mimicry; raucous laughter
KNOWN COMPANIONS: Hondo Ohnaka, Turk Falso

PILF MUKMUK
PIRATE'S PET

Tufted crest tended to by Hondo

Wide mouth has no teeth

Carefully groomed neck ruff

Long arms are ideal for stealing things

WITH DOOKU

Count Dooku has endured some bad days in his long life, but this one may be the worst: His ship has crashed on Vanqor, he's surrounded by scruffy pirates with guns pointed at him, and now a Kowakian monkey-lizard is rummaging through his pockets. What would they say in the grand drawing rooms of Serenno?

A STERN JEDI WITH a rigid sense of right and wrong, Plo Koon believes the Separatists must be opposed at all costs. Yet he cares deeply for the troops under his command, and risks his own life at Abregado in an effort to save theirs.

PLO KOON
THE BLADE OF DORIN

Oxygen is poison to Kel Dor

Heat-resistant Jedi robes

BRAVE STAND

Plo Koon's thick skin allows him to survive for several minutes even in a freezing vacuum. After the Jedi Cruiser *Triumphant* is destroyed by the *Malevolence*, Plo defends his men by leaving their escape pod to fight General Grievous's battle droids, making his stand in the darkness of space.

Forearm armor from fallen clone

Lightsaber held to warn foes

STATISTICS

SPECIES: Kel Dor
HEIGHT: 1.88 m (6 ft 2 in)
GENDER: Male
ALLEGIANCE: Jedi Order
HOMEWORLD: Dorin
WEAPONS: Lightsaber
TALENTS: Lightsaber combat; Force sensitivity; expert pilot
KNOWN COMPANIONS: Yoda, Kit Fisto, Ahsoka Tano, Commander Wolffe, Boost, Sinker

PLUNK DROIDS GET THEIR name in imitation of their rather rudimentary droidspeak. These plodding droids exist to refuel ships and equipment and perform simple tasks in spaceports and military bases. Their thick hulls house tanks filled with volatile liquid tibanna.

STATISTICS

SPECIES: Power droid
HEIGHT: 1.37 m (4 ft 6 in)
GENDER: None programmed
ALLEGIANCE: Neutral
MANUFACTURER: Industrial Automaton
WEAPONS: None
EQUIPMENT: Power couplings, fuel tanks

Thick shielding over fuel reservoir

Fuel hose links to thirsty ships

Main panel for system diagnostics

Feet allow droid to waddle along

HAVE TIBANNA, WILL FLY

Most starships use fusion generators to power their systems. But some, such as Y-wing bombers, rely on liquid tibanna. Plunk droids refuel these craft, waddling from ship to ship as fast as their stubby legs will allow, while mumbling to themselves in droidspeak.

THE LEADER OF THE Geonosians and a key member of the Techno Union, Poggle is tireless in his efforts to aid the Separatists, hoping to turn his planet into a major galactic power. But by doing so, he risks the Republic discovering secrets about Geonosis.

POGGLE THE LESSER
ARCHDUKE OF GEONOSIS

Cranial ridges are sign of high caste

Wings rarely used since youth

Archduke's Staff of Command

SECRET WEAPONS

Once back in control of his great factories, Poggle immediately begins production of new weapons for use when the Republic again tries to occupy Geonosis. This time, he thinks, the addition of super tanks and tactical droids will mean victory.

STATISTICS

SPECIES: Geonosian
HEIGHT: 1.83 m (6 ft)
GENDER: Male
ALLEGIANCE: Separatists
HOMEWORLD: Geonosis
WEAPONS: None
TALENTS: Superb engineer; leadership; knowledge of military tactics
KNOWN COMPANIONS: Count Dooku, Karina the Great, Nute Gunray, Lott Dod, Rush Clovis

CC-0411, OR COMMANDER "PONDS," serves under Mace Windu, often on Coruscant overseeing the course of the war. This has left Ponds far from the front. He wears his frustration on the back of his helmet, where he's scrawled "Some Guys Have All the Luck."

Helmet marked with personal motto

Crossed DC-17 pistols

PONDS
WAITING FOR HIS CHANCE

STATISTICS

SPECIES: Human
HEIGHT: 1.83 m (6 ft)
GENDER: Male
ALLEGIANCE: Republic
HOMEWORLD: Kamino
WEAPONS: DC-17 pistols, DC-15 blaster rifle
TALENTS: Armed and unarmed combat; jetpack expertise; recon and military tactics; leadership
KNOWN COMPANIONS: Mace Windu, Admiral Kilian

ACTION

No one is happier than Ponds when Mace Windu is sent to Ryloth for the Republic's invasion of the Separatist-held planet. Ponds finally sees action at Nabat and Lessu, leading the troopers of Lightning Squadron against Wat Tambor's forces.

THE GOVERNOR OF CONCORDIA, Pre Vizsla assists Duchess Satine in trying to hunt down the remnants of the Death Watch and prevent a return to Mandalore's warlike ways. But he has secrets of his own.

PRE VIZSLA
MANDALORIAN ON A MISSION

Cape with clan markings

CLAN HONOR

The Vizsla clan includes renegades who have embraced the outmoded values of the Death Watch, but Pre is different—he is one of Satine's staunchest allies in tracking down the Death Watch. Or so Satine thinks. In fact, Vizsla is the Death Watch's leader and awaits his chance for revenge on "modern" Mandalore.

War helmet of Death Watch

Dark saber stolen from the Jedi during the Old Republic

Polished armor protects shins

STATISTICS

SPECIES: Human

HEIGHT: 1.83 m (6 ft)

GENDER: Male

ALLEGIANCE: Separatists

HOMEWORLD: Mandalore

WEAPONS: Darksaber, WESTAR-35 blaster pistol

TALENTS: Combat; leadership; diplomacy

KNOWN COMPANIONS: Duchess Satine Kryze, Tal Merrik

A DIGNIFIED DIPLOMAT, Prime Minister Almec is proud of Mandalore's success in renouncing its violent past, and resents those who associate his planet only with warrior clans. He sees himself as a servant of Mandalore's people as the planet pursues a bright future.

Dignified bearing helps in politics

Almec favors simple clothes

STATISTICS

SPECIES: Human
HEIGHT: 1.89 m (6 ft 2 in)
GENDER: Male
ALLEGIANCE: Mandalore
HOMEWORLD: Mandalore
WEAPONS: None
TALENTS: Diplomacy
KNOWN COMPANIONS:

Duchess Satine Kryze,

Pre Vizsla, Tal Merrik

Tall boots of well-worn leather

ALMEC'S DILEMMA

After the attempt on Satine's life is foiled, scouts discover that the Death Watch armies are ready for war. Almec is alarmed, but wary of telling the Republic of this development: The arrival of Republic troops could make Mandalore's people view the Death Watch as liberators, not terrorists.

PRIME MINISTER ALMEC
MODERN MANDALORIAN

Soul patch is kept immaculate

DC-15 has had a lot of use on Christophsis

PUNCH
CHRISTOPHSIS CLONE

STATISTICS

SPECIES: Human

HEIGHT: 1.83 m (6 ft)

GENDER: Male

ALLEGIANCE: Republic

HOMEWORLD: Kamino

WEAPONS: DC-15 blaster pistol

TALENTS: Combat

KNOWN COMPANIONS: Sketch, Slick, Gus, Jester, Chopper

NOT THE SARGE!

Punch finds it hard to believe that a transmission to the Separatists could have come from his squad's barracks—but that's nothing compared with his surprise on learning that the turncoat is Slick. Why would Sarge throw in with the tinnies?

Elaborate hairstyles are mark of royalty

YOUNG NEEYUTNEE IS THE newly elected Queen of Naboo, succeeding Jamillia as the Clone Wars rage throughout the galaxy. Neeyutnee relies heavily on Padmé Amidala to see Naboo through the latest Separatist threats.

Scar of Remembrance divides lower lip

STATISTICS

SPECIES: Human

HEIGHT: 1.69 m (5 ft 7 in)

GENDER: Female

ALLEGIANCE: Naboo

HOMEWORLD: Naboo

WEAPONS: None

TALENTS: Diplomacy; legislative strategy; leadership

KNOWN COMPANIONS: Captain Typho, Padmé Amidala

Simple robe made from Cyrene silk

QUEEN NEEYUTNEE
RULER OF NABOO

TROUBLE!

Neeyutnee may be young, but she has no illusions about the peril Separatist agents pose to her planet. When battle droids are found, she orders an immediate investigation, with security forces ready to act if further signs of trouble are uncovered.

RO-Z67 WAS CREATED TO give children loving care. But Darth Sidious's agents reprogrammed her to supervise the Sith Lord's cruel experiments on stolen Jedi infants. Two of these unfortunate RO droids work in the Mustafar complex.

Hand-held injection syringe

RO-Z67
DARK SIDE DAYCARE

Self-propelled saw for minor surgery

Tubing leads to medical canisters

STATISTICS

SPECIES: Nanny droid

HEIGHT: 1.69 m (5 ft 6 in)

GENDER: Female programming

ALLEGIANCE: Separatists

MANUFACTURER: Go-Corp/Utilitech

WEAPONS: None

FEATURES: Programmed for childcare; language abilities; first-aid database

KNOWN COMPANIONS:
Darth Sidious, Cad Bane

WICKED GAME

Darth Sidious hopes to turn Jedi children into an army skilled with the dark side of the Force. To that end, he has ordered RO-Z67 be transformed from a kindly nanny droid into a cruel medical robot that barely notices when her charges are frightened or unhappy.

Gyroscopic wheel for locomotion

A SPUNKY, LOYAL, STUBBORN astromech, R2-D2 serves Anakin Skywalker and has saved the impulsive Jedi from many dangers. Though not designed for combat, he seems to enjoy a good fight with battle droids, using his tools to trick and defeat his foes.

Primary radar photoreceptor

STATISTICS

SPECIES: Astromech droid
HEIGHT: 96 cm (3 ft 2 in)
GENDER: Male programming
ALLEGIANCE: Republic
MANUFACTURER: Industrial Automaton
WEAPONS: None
FEATURES: Starfighter piloting and maintenance; database for general repairs; behavioral quirks due to a lack of memory wipes
KNOWN COMPANIONS: Anakin Skywalker, Ahsoka Tano, C-3PO, Padmé Amidala, Obi-Wan Kenobi

Main heat exhaust

IN ENEMY HANDS

Anakin Skywalker refuses to erase R2's memory, considering the little droid's quirks part of his unique personality. As a result, R2's brain contains top-secret military information. When R2 falls into the hands of General Grievous, the Republic war effort is in great danger.

A FEISTY, PINK-PANELED astromech, "Katie" serves with the famed 501st Legion, often handling logistics. Katie and R2-D2 can often be heard trading electronic gossip about the latest happenings in the Republic fleet's droid pool.

R2-KT
501ST ASSISTANT

Radar eye and photoreceptor

DEBRIEFING

At Ryloth, Republic forces prepare for an attempt to smash through the Separatist blockade and free the planet. R2-KT joins the gaggle of pilots and clone troopers assembled on the hangar deck for a briefing about battle plans. Mechanicals and living beings will both have jobs to do once the shooting starts.

Primary system ventilation port

STATISTICS

SPECIES: Astromech droid
HEIGHT: 1.1 m (3 ft 7 in)
GENDER: Female programming
ALLEGIANCE: Republic
MANUFACTURER: Industrial Automaton
WEAPONS: None
FEATURES: Starfighter piloting and maintenance; database for general repairs; logistics programming
KNOWN COMPANIONS: R2-D2

Powerbus cables for mobility control

R3-S6, OR "GOLDIE," WAS assigned to Anakin Skywalker after the loss of R2-D2 at Bothawui, and seemed oddly prone to mistakes. His secret: He had been reprogrammed as a Separatist agent by saboteurs working at a Republic base on Milagro.

Dome carousel for auxiliary arms

High-power coupling for system recharge

STATISTICS

SPECIES: Astromech droid
HEIGHT: 1.1 m (3 ft 7 in)
GENDER: Male programming
ALLEGIANCE: Separatists
MANUFACTURER: Industrial Automaton
WEAPONS: None
FEATURES: Starfighter piloting and maintenance; database for repairs; espionage programming
KNOWN COMPANIONS: Ahsoka Tano, Anakin Skywalker, Captain Rex

R3-S6
GRIEVOUS'S AGENT

POOR GOLDIE

Mourning the loss of R2-D2, Anakin Skywalker can hardly bear the idea of working with another astromech droid. Ahsoka Tano tries to get her Master to give the new droid a chance, nicknaming him Goldie to go with Anakin's Republic call sign of Gold Leader. But Anakin is unmoved, particularly after R3-S6 makes a number of dangerous in-flight errors.

R4-P17 WAS DAMAGED AND REBUILT with a scavenged R2 dome by Anakin Skywalker as a gift for Obi-Wan Kenobi. R4 is a cautious astromech, making her a very good fit for the wise, patient Jedi Knight. She accompanies Obi-Wan to many worlds, often staying with his fighter.

R4-P17
OBI-WAN'S CO-PILOT

Probe housed within right-side carousel

Grasper arm extended from left-side carousel

Central leg for balance over uneven surfaces

STATISTICS

SPECIES: Astromech droid
HEIGHT: 96 cm (3 ft 2 in)
GENDER: Female programming
ALLEGIANCE: Republic
MANUFACTURER: Industrial Automaton
WEAPONS: None
FEATURES: Starfighter piloting and maintenance; database for general repairs
KNOWN COMPANIONS: Obi-Wan Kenobi, R2-D2

BACK OFF, THIEVES!

R4-P17 was captured when Geonosian warriors found Obi-Wan's fighter on the red sands of Geonosis, and it's not an experience she wants to endure again. On Tatooine, R4 has a clear message for a gang of Jawas: Get lost!

R6-H5 HAS SERVED KIT FISTO on many missions and tends to worry about his Master. Kit blames R6's anxiety on the fact that he is used for testing prototype functions for future droids and fears glitches in his programs.

Onboard logic function displays

STATISTICS

SPECIES: Astromech droid
HEIGHT: 96 cm (3 ft 2 in)
GENDER: Male programming
ALLEGIANCE: Republic
MANUFACTURER: Industrial Automaton
WEAPONS: None
FEATURES: Starfighter piloting and maintenance; database for repairs
KNOWN COMPANIONS: Kit Fisto

R6-H5
FUSSING OVER FISTO

NEW ARRIVALS

On Vassek's moon, R6-H5 waits for Kit Fisto to return, keeping his sensors trained on his surroundings and the space high above him. He quickly discovers trouble: Grievous's starfighter is headed for the moon. Even worse, Grievous's MagnaGuard servants have found Kit's fighter.

R7-A7 IS ASSIGNED TO Ahsoka Tano and shares his mistress's rash, aggressive habits. R7 is one of a group of Jedi droids whose prototype logic modules are designed to test new programs, though his body is that of an R2 unit.

Panel hides in-flight grasper

R7-A7
AHSOKA'S ASTROMECH

STATISTICS

SPECIES: Astromech droid

HEIGHT: 96 cm (3 ft 2 in)

GENDER: Male programming

ALLEGIANCE: Republic

MANUFACTURER: Industrial Automaton

WEAPONS: None

FEATURES: Starfighter piloting and maintenance; database for general repairs

KNOWN COMPANIONS: Ahsoka Tano

Housing holds main drive motor

BAD FEELING

R7-A7's advanced logical modules can process a huge amount of combat data and predict the outcome of numerous battle scenarios at the same time. But in space above Ryloth, not even R7's processors can find a way for the Republic to win—they're outnumbered. R7 just hopes Ahsoka realizes the same thing.

R7-D4 SERVES PLO KOON and takes pride in maintaining the fighter of a legendary Jedi pilot. Plo is fond of the droid and refuses to send him for memory wipes. That would erase his lively personality.

DROID DUEL

Fellow astromech R2-D2 once had a run-in with R7-D4: R7 was busy displaying tactical information to a roomful of Jedi, when R2 tried to take over, lacking the time to explain why. The two began pushing and shoving—with plenty of angry beeps—as the Jedi watched the argument in stunned surprise.

Reader socket for data cards

Fine manipulator arm extends when needed

R7-D4
PLO'S COMPANION

STATISTICS

SPECIES: Astromech droid
HEIGHT: 96 cm (3 ft 2 in)
GENDER: Male programming
ALLEGIANCE: Republic
MANUFACTURER: Industrial Automaton
WEAPONS: None
FEATURES: Starfighter piloting and maintenance; database for general repairs
KNOWN COMPANIONS: Plo Koon

ONE OF LIGHTNING SQUADRON'S most experienced ARF troopers, Razor joins Mace Windu for a number of dangerous tasks on Ryloth, trusting in his training and his beloved AT-RT. Nothing is certain in war, but they haven't let him down yet.

Visor improves trooper's vision

Extra-powerful comlink system

RAZOR
RYLOTH RUNNER

STATISTICS

SPECIES: Human
HEIGHT: 1.83 m (6 ft)
GENDER: Male
ALLEGIANCE: Republic
HOMEWORLD: Kamino
WEAPONS: DC-15 blaster pistol
TALENTS: Combat; AT-RT driving
KNOWN COMPANIONS: Stak, Mace Windu, Commander Cody, Tae Boon

DC-15 for use in ground fighting

MACE'S MEN
Razor and his squadronmate Stak were trained on Kamino before their first battle, but they have learned much more by fighting alongside Mace Windu. Where their Jedi General leads, Razor and Stak will follow.

STATISTICS

SPECIES: Battle droid
HEIGHT: 2.58 m (8 ft 6 in)
GENDER: No gender programming
ALLEGIANCE: Separatists
MANUFACTURER: Retail Caucus
WEAPONS: Blaster cannons
EQUIPMENT: Sensory antennae

Antennas detect motion overhead

Blank "face" has no sensors

Twin laser cannons

Spring-loaded legs aid surprise attacks

RETAIL DROID
BURIED TROUBLE

WHAT LIES BENEATH

On Christophsis, Ahsoka Tano learns how important it is for a Jedi to be aware of her surroundings when she runs afoul of a clutch of buried retail droids that attack her and Anakin. For the Padawan, it's nearly a fatal lesson.

CC-7567, KNOWN AS "REX," serves Anakin Skywalker. His gruff, no-nonsense ways make a good fit with Anakin's bravery and recklessness. Rex thinks little of rank—in his mind, experience is what matters during war. The question is whether you live long enough to get it.

Jaig Eyes are a combat honor

Rex likes the speed of twin pistols

REX
CAPTAIN OF THE 501ST

STATISTICS

SPECIES: Human
HEIGHT: 1.83 m (6 ft)
GENDER: Male
ALLEGIANCE: Republic
HOMEWORLD: Kamino
WEAPONS: DC-17 pistols, DC-15 blaster rifle
TALENTS: Armed and unarmed combat; jetpack expertise; knowledge of recon and military tactics; leadership
KNOWN COMPANIONS: Anakin Skywalker, Ahsoka Tano, R2-D2, Obi-Wan Kenobi, Commander Cody

Holster is cut for quick-draw

CAPTAIN'S CHOICE

Rex has seen the deaths of too many troopers and Jedi to think that there's anything glorious about war. Yet his loyalty to the Republic and his fellow troopers hasn't wavered. Even if he hadn't been born to serve, how could he abandon his brothers and friends?

STATISTICS

SPECIES: Human
HEIGHT: 1.83 m (6 ft)
GENDER: Male
ALLEGIANCE: Republic
HOMEWORLD: Kamino
WEAPONS: Stun baton
TALENTS: Crowd control
EQUIPMENT: Riot shield, comlink

WAR AND UNREST ARE not unknown even on the capital of Coruscant. To keep peace on the home front, the Republic depends on riot clone troopers who are given special training in controlling crowds with shows of authority and the use of nonlethal weapons.

Stun baton gives nonlethal jolt

Riot shield of tough plastoid

RIOT CLONE TROOPER
PLANETARY PEACEKEEPERS

KEEPING ORDER

Riot-trooper squads are always at the ready in barracks spread across the cityscape of Coruscant, waiting for orders to deploy in case of trouble. They also help the capital's regular police when needed, supplying backup or helping in the hunt for dangerous fugitives.

RISHI EELS DWELL IN THE chilly tunnels and caverns that honeycomb the Rishi Moon. They are stealthy and rarely seen, leading some to dismiss them as tall tales. But they are very real—and very deadly.

Light-sensitive cluster of eyes

RISHI EEL
HUNTER IN THE SHADOWS

Mouthparts stretch to swallow prey

STATISTICS

SPECIES: Rishi Eel

LENGTH: 3.5 m (11 ft 6 in)

HOMEWORLD: Rishi Moon

WEAPONS: Bite; ability to swallow whole

ECOLOGY: Rishi eels dwell in the caves of the Rishi Moon, waiting to snatch unwary prey

Beak is used to dig out tunnels

Armored segments protect body

NIGHT HUNTER

After the rookies on Rishi Moon are forced to evacuate their base, they gather on the surface to figure out their next move, unaware that a Rishi eel has emerged from its warren of tunnels and is creeping ever closer. A lightning-quick strike and Cutup is carried off!

A YOUNG SENATOR FROM PANTORA, Riyo Chuchi lets Chairman Cho negotiate on behalf of their people. But Cho's apparent hunger for war with the Talz convinces Riyo that she must speak up for peace.

Traditional Pantoran headdress

Wrap with Senatorial epaulets

Gauntlets for cold weather

STATISTICS

SPECIES: Pantoran
HEIGHT: 1.65 m (5 ft 5 in)
GENDER: Female
ALLEGIANCE: Pantora
HOMEWORLD: Pantora
WEAPONS: None
TALENTS: Diplomacy; leadership
KNOWN COMPANIONS: Chi Cho

Decorated greaves

A DIPLOMATIC LESSON

With Chairman Cho dying, Riyo Chuchi turns to the Jedi in hopes that they can prevent further violence between the Pantorans and the Talz. But Obi-Wan Kenobi councils otherwise: This is Pantora's problem. Riyo gathers herself and approaches the Talz chieftain Thi-Sen. But unlike Cho, she treats him as an equal deserving respect.

THIS DIMINUTIVE BOUNTY hunter is skilled at slicing into computer networks and handling demolitions. Though small, he is quite capable—even capable of taking down an unwary Jedi. Judge Robonino by his size and you'll soon regret it.

Fins expand when angry or alarmed

Box of explosives for Cad Bane's plot

ROBONINO
SENATE SABOTEUR

STATISTICS

SPECIES: Patrolian
HEIGHT: 1.26 m (4 ft 2 in)
GENDER: Male
ALLEGIANCE: Himself
HOMEWORLD: Patrolia
WEAPONS: Shocker
TALENTS: Slicing; demolitions
KNOWN COMPANIONS: Aurra Sing, Shahan Alama, Cad Bane, HELIOS-3D

JEDI DOWN!

Anakin Skywalker is a dangerous opponent: Even without his lightsaber, he destroys one of Cad Bane's war droids and disarms Shahan Alama. But wily Robonino succeeds where his fellow hunters fail. He waits until the Jedi is distracted, then strikes quickly from behind.

ROCKET BATTLE DROIDS are modified with a jetpack to move through space. Grievous dispatches them to hunt survivors of the *Triumphant*, find their escape pods, and cut them open so the men die in space. It's a task the droids take to with chilling enthusiasm.

STATISTICS

SPECIES: Battle droid
HEIGHT: 1.91 m (6 ft 3 in)
GENDER: Male programming
ALLEGIANCE: Separatists
MANUFACTURER: Baktoid
WEAPONS: E-5 blaster rifle
EQUIPMENT: Head-mounted floodlamp, rocket pack, laser cutters

Head-mounted lamp for exploring debris

Built-in laser cutters

Rocket pack for use in space

Bright coloring for high visibility

ROCKET BATTLE DROID
VOID ASSASSIN

HUNTERS OF CLONES

The Abregado system is choked with debris that will take a long time to search. But Grievous's rocket droids know they can afford to take their time. Even if a Republic ship does arrive, it will be easy prey for the *Malevolence*'s deadly weapons.

THE SQUIRMY, STINKY SON OF Jabba the Hutt, little Rotta is Huttnapped as part of a Separatist plot to discredit the Jedi and broker an agreement between Jabba's clan and Count Dooku. Taken away from Tatooine's heat, Rotta becomes dangerously ill and needs medical care.

ROTTA THE HUTTLET
JABBA'S PEDUNKEE MUFKIN

Hutt skin secretes lubricating slime

Immature tail will grow and thicken

Fingers cling to folds of a parent's hide

STATISTICS

SPECIES: Hutt
HEIGHT: 43 cm (1 ft 8 in)
GENDER: Male
ALLEGIANCE: Desilijic Kajidic
HOMEWORLD: Tatooine
WEAPONS: None
TALENTS: Family connections
KNOWN COMPANIONS:
Jabba the Hutt,
Anakin Skywalker,
Ahsoka Tano,
R2-D2

A HUTTLET'S ADVENTURE

Most Huttlets spend the first fifty years of their life maturing in a parent's brood pouch, but not Rotta: Jabba wanted his son to experience life in the galaxy early. Mission accomplished: Rotta returns to Tatooine squealing eagerly about the flash of laser fire and the hum of lightsabers. So what's the entertainment for tomorrow?

Chromed pistol for close encounters

A CHEERFUL BUT DEADLY MEMBER of Sugi's gang of mercenaries, Rumi is willing to fight for anyone who pays her price. She proves her valor on Felucia against attacking pirates, rallying Akira's villagers against those who would steal their crops.

STATISTICS

SPECIES: Frenk
HEIGHT: 2.15 m (7 ft 1 in)
GENDER: Female
ALLEGIANCE: Neutral
HOMEWORLD: Gorobei
WEAPONS: Customized blaster pistol, IQA-11 blaster rifle
TALENTS: Combat; leadership; sniper skills
KNOWN COMPANIONS: Sugi, Embo, Seripas

Faded Frenk military uniform

A LIFE SPENT IN BATTLE

Beneath Rumi's cheerfulness, her mind is always at work, sizing up situations and thinking about military strategy. Sugi has come to rely on her as second-in-command for her keen judgment and her easy way with potential customers.

Reinforced boots could use a shine

RUSH CLOVIS IS AN IMPORTANT member of the Banking Clan whom the Jedi suspect of Separatist ties. He hopes to rekindle a long-ago romance with Padmé Amidala, while continuing to serve Count Dooku.

Tattoos are mark of status on Scipio

Scipio fashions recall planet's warrior past

RUSH CLOVIS
SLIPPERY SENATOR

STATISTICS

SPECIES: Human

HEIGHT: 1.92 m (6 ft 4 in)

GENDER: Male

ALLEGIANCE: Separatist

HOMEWORLD: Scipio

WEAPONS: Deactivator hold-out pistol

TALENTS: Charm; legislative knowledge; political skills

KNOWN COMPANIONS: Padmé Amidala, Poggle the Lesser

Boots are decorated to look like armor

PLEASURE TRIP

Clovis impulsively invites Padmé to go with him to Cato Neimoidia, where he hopes to mix the business of funding a new droid factory for the Separatists with the pleasure of winning back her affections. But his fellow Senator has her own agenda—to discover if he's a traitor.

A TATTOOED MEMBER OF THE Coruscant Guard, Rys finally gets a chance at action when he's forced down on Rugosa. Yoda teaches him to find inspiration in his allies, rather than focus on enemies.

RYS
RECON ON RUGOSA

Standard-issue Republic pack

STATISTICS

SPECIES: Human
HEIGHT: 1.83 m (6 ft)
GENDER: Male
ALLEGIANCE: Republic
HOMEWORLD: Kamino
WEAPONS: DC-15 blaster pistol, DC-15 blaster rifle
TALENTS: Combat, recon, and military tactics
KNOWN COMPANIONS: Lieutenant Thire, Jek, Yoda

Thermal detonator clipped to belt

SHOWDOWN ON THE RIM

Rys has spent a good chunk of the war on Coruscant, escorting Senators and monitoring fleet movements in the Outer Rim. On Rugosa's coral moon, he finally has a chance to get up close and personal with the Separatists' clanker hordes.

DUCHESS SATINE KRYZE IS THE leader of Mandalore and a passionate voice for pacifism in the galaxy. But dark forces within her own society would like to see her silenced and will stop at nothing to do so. Satine accepts the possibility that she may have to die for her beliefs.

Headress recalls Mandalorian war helmet

Hair styled in Kalevalan manner

SATINE KRYZE
CONSCIENCE OF MANDALORE

STATISTICS

SPECIES: Human
HEIGHT: 1.77 m (5 ft 10 in)
GENDER: Female
ALLEGIANCE: Mandalore
HOMEWORLD: Kalevala
WEAPONS: Deactivator hold-out pistol
TALENTS: Leadership; diplomacy
KNOWN COMPANIONS: Obi-Wan Kenobi, Prime Minister Almec, Pre Vizsla, Kin Robb, Tal Merrik

Gown makes use of soothing colors

AN OLD BOND

When he was young, Obi-Wan so loved Satine that he would have left the Jedi Order if she'd asked him to—and she loved him. A lot has happened since then, but the Jedi and the Duchess still have feelings for each other.

Blue is traditional color of the Guard

THE BEST AND BRAVEST MEMBERS of the famed Senate Guards are selected to become Commandos, carrying out secret missions on Coruscant as well as elsewhere in the galaxy. Their proud tradition is one of the most cherished in the Republic they serve.

Shoulder bell used in rifle work

Black body glove similar to clone trooper's

SENATE COMMANDO
BEST OF "THE BLUE WALL"

STATISTICS

SPECIES: Human

HEIGHT: Varies

GENDER: Male

ALLEGIANCE: Republic

HOMEWORLD: Coruscant

WEAPONS: DC-15 blaster pistol, DC-15 blaster rifle

EQUIPMENT: Helmet, armor, communications gear

DEFENDERS OF THE SENATE

The Senate Guard has protected the galaxy's legislators for centuries: Their blue robes and crested helmets are reassuring sights on Coruscant. The bravest Guardsmen become Senate Commandos, donning blue armor to tackle covert assignments.

Seripas looks ferocious—a hulking figure in armor who has clearly seen plenty of combat. As Ahsoka Tano finds out, the truth is a bit different: That imposing armor is controlled by a tiny being who is hiding inside it.

SERIPAS
LESS THAN MEETS THE EYE

Helmet hides Seripas's identity

Massive fist can scar durasteel

STATISTICS

SPECIES: Unknown

HEIGHT: in armor: 2.06 m (6 ft 9 in); without armor: 74 cm (2 ft 5 in)

GENDER: Male

ALLEGIANCE: Neutral

HOMEWORLD: Unknown

WEAPONS: Armored exoskeleton

TALENTS: Combat; exoskeleton operation

KNOWN COMPANIONS: Sugi, Embo, Rumi Paramita

RETHINKING HIS STRATEGY

When Hondo's gang attacks the village, Seripas finds he can't move quickly enough to fight the pirates on their speeder bikes. His armor is intimidating, but too bulky for this kind of fight. Perhaps it's time that he shed his beloved exoskeleton.

LIFE ON THE FARM HAS been good to young Shaeeah—there are chores to do, but also time to play. However, strange things are happening on Saleucami, and Shaeeah's quiet life is about to change. It all begins with the arrival of a mysterious stranger.

TWO MEN, ONE FACE

Shaeeah doesn't understand why the armored stranger in the barn has the same face as her stepfather. But her parents taught her never to turn away those in need, and the man with the familiar face needs help.

Simple dress sewn by her mother

Wrappings keep out dust and mud

SHAEEAH LAWQUANE

A GIRL FAR FROM THE WAR

STATISTICS

SPECIES: Human/Twi'lek

HEIGHT: 1.15 m (3 ft 9 in)

GENDER: Female

ALLEGIANCE: Neutral

HOMEWORLD: Saleucami

WEAPONS: None

TALENTS: Farming

KNOWN COMPANIONS:

Suu Lawquane, Jek Lawquane, Cut Lawquane, Captain Rex

A LEATHERY WEEQUAY WHO WEARS a jaunty red beret, Shahan Alama joined Cad Bane's posse of bounty hunters after being kicked out of a gang of pirates—for being too nasty. With Cad Bane's crew, there's no such thing as too nasty.

Favorite beret saved from pirate days

Combat droid's arm grafted onto elbow

SHAHAN ALAMA
WEEQUAY STALKER

STATISTICS

SPECIES: Weequay
HEIGHT: 1.85 m (6 ft 1 in)
GENDER: Male
ALLEGIANCE: Himself
HOMEWORLD: Sriluur
WEAPONS: LL-30 blaster pistol, blaster rifle, razor net
TALENTS: Gunman; expert tracker; capable pilot
KNOWN COMPANIONS: Aurra Sing, Robonino, Cad Bane, HELIOS-3D

Belt stolen from Twi'lek noble

Well-worn boots of nerf hide

SENATE SWEEP

Alama may have a bad reputation as a pirate, but he's a smart hunter: When he notices that a sentinel droid destroyed by Anakin Skywalker shows no signs of lightsaber cuts, he realizes a Jedi is on the loose—without his weapon.

A LONGTIME AIDE TO ONACONDA Farr, Rodia's Senator, Silood is always at Farr's side, taking care of his schedule and quietly offering advice when Farr wants a word with his old friend. Ono's fellow Senators have learned to value his thoughts, too.

Excellent hearing for use in hunting

Silk tunic allows for silent movement

Suction-cup fingers evolved for climbing

SILOOD
ONACONDA'S CONFIDANT

STATISTICS

SPECIES: Rodian

HEIGHT: 1.68 m (5 ft 6 in)

GENDER: Male

ALLEGIANCE: Onaconda Farr

HOMEWORLD: Rodia

WEAPONS: None

TALENTS: Logistics; legislative strategy; political savvy

KNOWN COMPANIONS: Onaconda Farr, Lolo Purs, Padmé Amidala

FAITHFUL SERVANT

Silood disagrees with Onaconda Farr's decision to hand Padmé Amidala over to Nute Gunray in return for the food their starving planet needs. He knows better than to trust a Neimoidian—when's the last time one of them kept a promise?

SINKER ESCAPES THE DESTRUCTION of the *Triumphant* along with Plo Koon, Wolffe, and Boost. He leaves their crowded escape pod to mow down rocket battle droids with his trusty DC-15 and a timely Force push from Plo Koon.

SINKER
SERGEANT IN SPACE

Wolfpack insignia has become famous

Wolffe chose unit's rusty red colors

Charge magazine for DC-15 blaster

STATISTICS

SPECIES: Human
HEIGHT: 1.83 m (6 ft)
GENDER: Male
ALLEGIANCE: Republic
HOMEWORLD: Kamino
WEAPONS: DC-15 blaster pistol
TALENTS: Combat
KNOWN COMPANIONS: Boost, Commander Wolffe, Plo Koon

INTO THE VOID

Clone troopers practice fighting in zero gravity, but few ever get the chance to do so: If you're ever floating alone in deep space, something has gone badly wrong with your mission. But a wise soldier never says never, so Sinker finds himself exiting his escape pod to hunt battle droids against the black backdrop of deep space.

A BRILLIANT REPUBLIC SCIENTIST, Sionver Boll's electron bomb turns the tide in the battle for Malastare. But she wonders about the morality of killing the Zillo Beast for the war effort. The creature may be the last of its kind—is it right to take its life?

Eyes indicate aquatic ancestry

Datapad filled with scientific notes

Insignia of military's Science Division

Uniform is dirty from long lab nights

STATISTICS

SPECIES: Unknown
HEIGHT: 1.73 m (5 ft 8 in)
GENDER: Female
ALLEGIANCE: Republic
HOMEWORLD: Unknown
WEAPONS: None
TALENTS: Engineering; biology; weapons construction
KNOWN COMPANIONS: Doge Nakha Urus, the Zillo Beast, Chancellor Palpatine, Mas Amedda

DOCTOR'S ORDERS

It was Dr. Boll herself who suggested that the Zillo Beast's strong, lightweight scales could prove useful for researching new clone armor. But she never imagined Chancellor Palpatine would order her to cause the creature terrible pain—or to kill it in the name of science.

SKALDERS ARE BIG, DUMB beasts that munch grass in the shadow of Florrum's geysers. They can sense when eruptions are near, and break into a lumbering trot to avoid painful burns from the acid sprays.

STATISTICS

SPECIES: Skalder
HEIGHT: 3.5 m (11 ft 6 in)
HOMEWORLD: Florrum
WEAPONS: Sharp tusks
ECOLOGY: Skalders are thick-skinned, placid herbivores who dwell on the plains of Florrum

SKALDER
FOUR-LEGGED FLORRUMITES

Clone trooper pursuing pirates

Thick hides offer protection

Long tusks for digging up roots

GIDDYUP!

Desperate to catch up with Hondo's pirates, Jar Jar Binks and the clone troopers under Commander Stone leap aboard skalders, kicking the big creatures' sides until they finally break into a lumbering run. The skalders may look clumsy, but they move with surprising speed.

A TATTOOED MEMBER OF Slick's squad, Sketch's keen observation skills help Cody and Rex eliminate suspects and zero in on the real traitor within the Christophis base. He catches Chopper telling a lie—he wasn't in the mess hall like he claims, but is he the traitor?

DC-15 ready for action

Tattoo'ed letter "S" for "Sketch"

A BROTHER'S BETRAYAL

Sketch is as surprised as his squadmates when the traitor turns out to be their own sergeant, Slick. The clones are a band of brothers, and how could anyone betray such a connection?

SKETCH
TROOPER IN TROUBLE

Greaves dingy with grime from combat

STATISTICS

SPECIES: Human

HEIGHT: 1.83 m (6 ft)

GENDER: Male

ALLEGIANCE: Republic

HOMEWORLD: Kamino

WEAPONS: DC-15 blaster pistol

TALENTS: Trained for combat

KNOWN COMPANIONS: Punch, Sergeant Slick, Gus, Hawk, Jester, Chopper

CLONE TROOPERS HAVE TO be able to think for themselves to be good soldiers, and Slick has done a lot of thinking —enough to conclude that clones are simply slaves for the Jedi. He can therefore no longer serve the Republic's war machine.

Familiar features hide radical thoughts

SLICK
SEPARATIST SYMPATHIZER

STATISTICS

SPECIES: Human
HEIGHT: 1.83 m (6 ft)
GENDER: Male
ALLEGIANCE: Separatists
HOMEWORLD: Kamino
WEAPONS: DC-15 blaster pistol
TALENTS: Combat; leadership
KNOWN COMPANIONS:
Punch, Sketch, Gus, Hawk,
Jester, Chopper

DC-15 will be used against the Republic

CAUGHT

Once his plan to frame one of his men as the traitor fails, Slick begins to sweat: He has to outthink two specially trained clones in Commander Cody and Captain Rex. Slick is determined to outfox them. But two heads prove better than one.

A SKILLED ARF TROOPER, STAK is one of the first to make contact with Cham Syndulla's rebels when he strikes up a friendly rivalry with Tae Boon and his band of Twi'lek blurrg riders on the way to Lessu.

Visor circuitry enhances vision

DC-15's folding stock can be extended

Boots reinforced against vibration

STATISTICS

SPECIES: Human
HEIGHT: 1.83 m (6 ft)
GENDER: Male
ALLEGIANCE: Republic
HOMEWORLD: Kamino
WEAPONS: DC-15 blaster pistol
TALENTS: AT-RT piloting; combat
KNOWN COMPANIONS: Razor, Mace Windu, Commander Cody, Tae Boon

STAK
LIGHTNING LEAPER

BRIDGE OUT

After a terrifying trip into Lessu, Stak and Razor fight to reactivate the plasma bridge leading into the Twi'lek city so their fellow clone troopers and Twi'lek guerillas can join the fight against the Separatists.

CC-5869, NICKNAMED "STONE," SERVES IN the Coruscant Guard. He is often attached to the Diplomatic Escort Group, which guards senior Republic officials on dangerous missions to worlds near the front lines of the civil war with Dooku's Separatists.

Doubts about best chain of command

Colors of the Coruscant Guard

STONE
FLORRUM FIGHTER

STATISTICS

SPECIES: Human
HEIGHT: 1.83 m (6 ft)
GENDER: Male
ALLEGIANCE: Republic
HOMEWORLD: Kamino
WEAPONS: DC-17 pistols, DC-15 blaster rifle
TALENTS: Armed and unarmed combat; jetpack expertise; knowledge of recon and military tactics; leadership
KNOWN COMPANIONS: Commander Fox, Jar Jar Binks, Senator Kharrus

JAR JAR'S ORDERS

Stone's troops think the idea of taking orders from a Gungan is ridiculous: How is Jar Jar Binks going to lead a fight against Florrum's space pirates? Stone agrees, but he will still follow the chain of command—so Representative Binks is in charge here.

SUGI AND HER GANG ARE paid muscle who protect Felucian farmers against pirates intent on stealing their crops. Sugi considers this honorable work—and is determined to protect her clients even if it costs her and her gang their lives.

STATISTICS

SPECIES: Zabrak
HEIGHT: 1.83 m (6 ft)
GENDER: Female
ALLEGIANCE: Neutral
HOMEWORLD: Iridonia
WEAPONS: EE-3 blaster rifle, vibroblade
TALENTS: Armed and unarmed combat; piloting
KNOWN COMPANIONS: Embo, Seripas, Rumi Paramita

Hair kept out of way in topknot

Strength built up over years of fighting

SUGI
A HUNTER WITH HONOR

Vibroblade for close combat

SHOWDOWN ON FELUCIA

Sugi is angry when her honor is questioned by Obi-Wan Kenobi, but she grows to respect him and his Jedi companions. Obi-Wan, in turn, realizes that Sugi is more than just your typical vibroblade for hire.

Sugi is fast and agile in a fight

BIG, DUMB, AND tough, B2 battle droids are the muscle of the Separatist infantry. Their simple programming makes them very aggressive, sometimes shoving B1 droids aside in their haste to attack. Some B1s call their bigger cousins "sir" or "boss."

B2-HA series droid equipped with missile firing arm

Main systems status indicator

Flexi-armor midsection

SUPER BATTLE DROID
MECHANICAL MUSCLE

THE THICK BLUE LINE

Super battle droids often march ahead of other Separatist units, with B1s acting as snipers while using supers' thick blue-durasteel armor as cover. Clone troopers often combat supers with pulses from EMP grenades, known on the battlefield as "droid poppers." While their systems reboot, the paralyzed B2s can be destroyed.

STATISTICS

SPECIES: Battle droid
HEIGHT: 1.93 m (6 ft 4 in)
GENDER: Male programming
ALLEGIANCE: Separatists
MANUFACTURER: Baktoid
WEAPONS: Wrist-mounted laser cannon
EQUIPMENT: Sensors, communications suite

Hidden vanes vent heat in the system

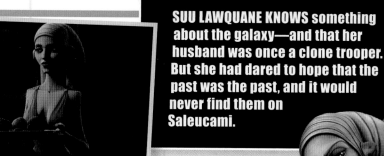

SUU LAWQUANE KNOWS something about the galaxy—and that her husband was once a clone trooper. But she had dared to hope that the past was the past, and it would never find them on Saleucami.

HOSPITALITY

When clone troopers arrive on Suu's farm, her first instinct is to warn them away at blaster point. Seeing a wounded man among them, however, she can't turn them away.

Antique Twi'lek hunting rifle

STATISTICS

SPECIES: Twi'lek
HEIGHT: 1.85 m (6 ft 1 in)
GENDER: Female
ALLEGIANCE: Neutral
HOMEWORLD: Saleucami
WEAPONS: Blaster rifle
TALENTS: Farming
KNOWN COMPANIONS: Cut Lawquane, Jek Lawquane, Shaeeah Lawquane

SUU LAWQUANE
A FARMER'S WIFE

Coverall worn over work pants

HOME INVASION

Suu can take care of herself. But when a squad of commando droids attacks the farm, she leaves the fighting to Cut and Captain Rex, protecting her children and hoping the two clones can prevail.

A MEMBER OF the ill-fated Blue Squadron, Swoop pilots a V-19 Torrent starfighter at Ryloth and is caught in the deadly ambush planned by Mar Tuuk. He is the only member of his fighter group to make it back to the *Resolute*.

Polarized T-visor with glare filter

Breastplate slides over abdomen armor

SWOOP
PILOT IN PERIL

STATISTICS

SPECIES: Human
HEIGHT: 1.83 m (6 ft)
GENDER: Male
ALLEGIANCE: Republic
HOMEWORLD: Kamino
WEAPONS: DC-15 blaster pistol
TALENTS: Fighter piloting; military tactics
KNOWN COMPANIONS: Ahsoka Tano, Kickback, Slammer, Axe, Tucker

VULTURES!

Swoop commands Blue Squadron's second fighter group at Ryloth, taking orders from Ahsoka. Testing the Separatist blockade, he is horrified to see his targeting computer light up with new contacts—vulture droids everywhere!

PROGRAMMED FOR SOPHISTICATED military and combat strategy, tactical droids are smart but argumentative, often debating with their Separatist leaders. Organics make too many errors, and should leave the science of war to mechanicals.

Tactical droids have individual color schemes

STATISTICS

SPECIES: Battle droid
HEIGHT: 1.93 m (6 ft 4 in)
GENDER: Male programming
ALLEGIANCE: Separatists
MANUFACTURER: Baktoid
WEAPONS: E-5 blaster rifle
EQUIPMENT: Armor, sophisticated strategic analysis software

Precise digits for console input

THE NUMBERS

TX-20 leads the defense of the Twi'lek city of Nabat on behalf of Wat Tambor, protecting his proton cannons with Twi'lek and releasing gutkurrs to hunt refugees. His droid brain tells him it's a flawless strategy, but Obi-Wan Kenobi and his troops prove him wrong.

CHAM SYNDULLA'S SECOND-IN-COMMAND, Tae Boon is a respected leader in his own right. He is an expert blurrg rider, with a natural gift for getting the fierce beasts to understand and obey his commands.

Antique Twi'lek war helmet

Stripped-down DL-44 pistol

TAE BOON
THE BLURRG WHISPERER

STATISTICS

SPECIES: Twi'lek
HEIGHT: 1.85 m (6 ft 1 in)
GENDER: Male
ALLEGIANCE: Cham Syndulla
HOMEWORLD: Ryloth
WEAPONS: DL-44 blaster pistol
TALENTS: Blurrg riding; expert marksman; leadership
KNOWN COMPANIONS: Cham Syndulla, Gobi Glie

Trousers made of rough twill

MISERY ON RYLOTH

When the Separatists invade, Tae Boon prepares to fight in order to stop them stripping Ryloth of valuables. But Wat Tambor has not come just to steal—his goal is to destroy the Twi'lek people as a lesson to the Republic.

Snood of rich
Kalevalan cloth

TAL MERRIK, THE Senator from Kalevala, is
known for his talent as a peacemaker
and for his friendship with the
pacifist Duchess Satine. But Merrik
has a secret. When he reveals it, the
galaxy will once more respect the
warrior traditions of Mandalore.

Fingers knit
as Tal bides
his time

TAL MERRIK
MANDALORIAN MOLE

STATISTICS

SPECIES: Human
HEIGHT: 1.85 m (6 ft 1 in)
GENDER: Male
ALLEGIANCE: Separatists
HOMEWORLD: Kalevala
WEAPONS: LL-30 blaster pistol
TALENTS: Weapons handling;
legislative knowledge;
diplomacy
KNOWN COMPANIONS: Duchess
Satine Kryze, Kin Robb, Orn
Free Taa, Pre Vizsla

A FRIEND BETRAYED

Aboard the *Coronet*, Merrik
seizes his chance to strike.
He will kidnap Duchess Satine
and deliver her to Pre Vizsla,
leader of the secretive
Death Watch cult. Then, in
league with the Separatists,
he and Vizsla will restore the
honor of the Mandalorians.

TAN DIVO
CONCEITED INSPECTOR

INSPECTOR LIEUTENANT TAN DIVO is sent to discover who killed a Rodian Senator. It's not an assignment that excites the inspector: Dealing with Senators guarantees Divo will have to file lots of reports.

Hairstyle shows Divo is hardly a slave to fashion

Comlink delivers new developments

Stripes indicate hard-earned rank

Republic insignia demands respect

Multiple datapads full of reports

STATISTICS

SPECIES: Human
HEIGHT: 1.8 m (5 ft 11 in)
GENDER: Male
ALLEGIANCE: Republic
HOMEWORLD: Coruscant
WEAPONS: A-43 Hushabye pistol
TALENTS: Running investigations; filling out police reports

TOUGH CASE

On his mission to discover who killed Senator Onaconda Farr, Inspector Lieutenant Tan Divo must follow a trail of strange clues. Was it a Kaminoan with access to poison? Or was the killer someone else?

POWERFUL JABBA THE HUTT refuses to speak to his visitors in anything but Huttese, so he requires translators. TC-70 is the latest to hold this perilous job: Jabba tends to blame the translator when he hears news that he dislikes.

Photoreceptors glow when active

Olfactory sensor is currently deactivated

Speech generator beneath mouth slot

Exterior plating covers components

STATISTICS

SPECIES: Protocol droid
HEIGHT: 1.67 m (5 ft 6 in)
GENDER: Female programming
ALLEGIANCE: Desilijic Kajidic
MANUFACTURER: Cybot Galactica
WEAPONS: None
FEATURES: Programmed for diplomacy; fluent in many forms of communication; knowledge of species' cultures
KNOWN COMPANIONS: Jabba the Hutt, Rotta the Huttlet

SO MANY MEETINGS

In his time serving Jabba the Hutt, TC-70 has had to interpret for beings scary enough to melt her circuits: If it's not pirates, it's bounty hunters or slavers. But after Rotta's kidnapping, Tatooine sees a parade of different visitors, all of whom wear lightsabers. Something tells TC-70 that they're the most dangerous guests of all.

Jabba is tired of gaudy paint job

AN ADVOCATE OF THE PACIFIST philosophy of Te Padka, Tee Watt Kaa persuades his followers to leave Mygeeto for Maridun. When war finds his colony, he refuses to back away from his belief that war destroys all it touches, corrupting even those who fight only when attacked.

TEE WATT KAA
LURMEN LEADER

STATISTICS

SPECIES: Lurmen
HEIGHT: 1.03 m (3 ft 5 in)
GENDER: Male
ALLEGIANCE: Neutral
HOMEWORLD: Maridun
WEAPONS: None
TALENTS: Leadership; debate
KNOWN COMPANIONS: Wag Too

Beard stiffened with apis wax

Robe of coarse dyed cloth

Sandals made of phalone hide

A FAMILY QUARREL

Tee Watt Kaa has always imagined that his son Wag Too will follow in his footsteps, learning the peaceful lessons of Te Padka and leading the Lurmen colony when Tee's time is past. But when the Separatists arrive, Wag struggles to accept his father's pacifist ways.

JEDI TERA SINUBE IS AN expert on the criminal underworld of Coruscant, and a skilled sleuth. The Force helps him solve crimes, but Sinube is also a master at reading people and thinking a step ahead of them. Even for a Jedi, the best tools are often the eyes, ears, and brain.

Lightsaber hilt made of Cosian wood

Saber hilt fits into top of Tera's cane

TERA SINUBE
JEDI INVESTIGATOR

STATISTICS

SPECIES: Cosian
HEIGHT: 1.83 m (6 ft)
GENDER: Male
ALLEGIANCE: Jedi Order
HOMEWORLD: Cosia
WEAPONS: Sabercane
TALENTS: Lightsaber combat; force sensitivity; interrogations; sleuthing; underworld knowledge
KNOWN COMPANIONS: Ahsoka Tano, Jocasta Nu, Yoda

Cosians' legs have "extra" knee

OLD AND WISE

Tera and Ahsoka Tano have a chance to catch up with thieves Cassie Cryar and Ione Marcy at an airtrain station. So why is Sinube driving so slowly? Because, he explains, he put a tracker on Ione: If you plan ahead, haste is rarely necessary—usually it just leads to mistakes.

A TRIBAL CHIEF OF ORTO Plutonia's Talz, Thi-Sen wants only for his people to be left alone. But when their home is invaded, he takes up arms and fights fiercely against the trespassers. If they insist on rejecting his offer of peace, then he will bring them war.

Crest made from narglatch spine

Smaller eyes used in bright light

Spear made of sharpened bone

THI-SEN
SON OF THE SUNS

STATISTICS

SPECIES: Talz
HEIGHT: 2.48 m (7 ft 2 in)
GENDER: Male
ALLEGIANCE: Talz
HOMEWORLD: Orto Plutonia
WEAPONS: Spear
TALENTS: Leadership; diplomacy; knowledge of clan traditions; combat skills; narglatch riding
KNOWN COMPANIONS: Medcha Wanto

A NEW CHANCE

When the Pantoran leader Chi Cho declares war on Thi-Sen's people, the Talz leads his clan to meet them on narglatches, destroying both Pantorans and clones. Further violence is avoided when Riyo Chuchi offers peace.

Thick claws can dig through ice

CC-4477, NICKNAMED "THIRE," SERVES
IN the Coruscant Guard and
accompanies Yoda to Rugosa.
Yoda urges the impatient young
lieutenant to think before rushing
into battle, reminding him that the
war will be long.

Shoulder
pauldron
worn by
officers

STATISTICS

SPECIES: Human
HEIGHT: 1.83 m (6 ft)
GENDER: Male
ALLEGIANCE: Republic
HOMEWORLD: Kamino
WEAPONS: DC-15 blaster
pistol, DC-15 blaster rifle
TALENTS: Combat, recon, and
military tactics; leadership
KNOWN COMPANIONS:
Yoda, Jek, Rys

Thire is an
expert with
DC-15 rifle

Colors of the
Coruscant Guard

THIRE

WOUNDED ON RUGOSA

AMBUSHED!

Escaping a Separatist ambush,
Lieutenant Thire and troopers Rys and
Jek find themselves facing an entire
Separatist battalion on the coral moon
of Rugosa. Despite long odds, Yoda
assures the squad that they will prevail.

AN ANXIOUS TECHNO-SERVICE droid, Todo 360 infiltrates the Jedi Temple on the orders of his master, Cad Bane. Todo is a worrywart and reacts angrily when Bane asks him to do menial tasks. Does he look like a butler?

TODO 360
STEALTHY SERVICE DROID

Cranium contains sensor suite

DESCENT INTO THE TEMPLE

Todo 360 accompanies Cad Bane into the Jedi Temple to steal a holocron; a tough job made harder by the grouchy bounty hunter's constant abuse. Bane doesn't seem to understand that slicing into the Jedi's computer systems is a challenge even for a techno-service droid as sophisticated as Todo.

Primary system power unit

STATISTICS

SPECIES: Service droid
HEIGHT: 66 cm (2 ft 2 in)
GENDER: Male programming
ALLEGIANCE: Neutral
MANUFACTURER: Vertseth Automata
WEAPONS: None
TALENTS: Errand-running; infiltration
KNOWN COMPANIONS: Cad Bane, Cato Parasitti

Repulsorlifts in dislike feet

KING KATUUNKO'S TOYDARIAN guards have largely ceremonial duties, but still carry blaster rifles in case the monarch needs their help. Alas, such weapons are of little use against Asajj Ventress's Force powers or her legion of battle droids.

Flexible nose resembles trunk

Wings can beat ten times a second

WAIT AND SEE

When King Katuunko's guards see the firepower Asajj Ventress has brought with her on the coral moon of Rugosa, they know that they have little chance of keeping the King safe long enough to escape in his space yacht. But their liege doesn't seem worried, and so the guards wait to see what will happen.

Blaster rifle with sniper scope

TOYDARIAN GUARD
KATUUNKO'S BODYGUARDS

STATISTICS

SPECIES: Toydarian

HEIGHT: 1.41 m (4 ft 7 in)

GENDER: Male

ALLEGIANCE: King Katuunko

HOMEWORLD: Toydaria

WEAPONS: Ubrikkian Arms L60 blaster rifle

EQUIPMENT: Sensors, macrobinoculars, communications gear

Toes rarely touch ground while on duty

TRENCH WAS BELIEVED killed at the Battle of Malastare Narrows, but the eight-limbed alien admiral survived. The mere sight of his deadly Dreadnaught, *Invincible*, is enough to fill veteran Republic officers with fear.

TRENCH
LEGENDARY COMMANDER

Mandibles kept neatly groomed

A WORTHY OPPONENT

At Christophsis, Trench traps Bail Organa on the surface and waits for the Republic to rescue him. He is delighted when Anakin Skywalker enters the battle in a stealth ship. It's been so long since Trench got to face a worthy adversary.

Pointer doubles as swagger stick

STATISTICS

SPECIES: Harch
HEIGHT: 1.89 m (6 ft 2 in)
GENDER: Male
ALLEGIANCE: Separatists
HOMEWORLD: Secundus Ando
WEAPONS: None
TALENTS: Military tactics; leadership
KNOWN COMPANIONS: Count Dooku

Rear legs adapted for walking upright

A PILOT FOR THE REPUBLIC'S Blue Squadron, clone soldier Tucker bravely flies his V-19 fighter into a cloud of vulture droids above Ryloth, though he knows the odds aren't good that he'll survive the fight. There are too many vulture droids out there, and too few V-19s.

Symbol of Blue Squadron

Arms held behind back while awaiting orders

STATISTICS

SPECIES: Human
HEIGHT: 1.83 m (6 ft)
GENDER: Male
ALLEGIANCE: Republic
HOMEWORLD: Kamino
WEAPONS: DC-15 blaster pistol
TALENTS: Expert fighter pilot; military tactics
KNOWN COMPANIONS: Ahsoka Tano, Kickback, Axe, Swoop

TUCKER
RYLOTH FLIGHT

DEADLY BEAUTY

The other pilots in Blue Squadron think Tucker is a bit crazy for saying so, but he has always found space combat beautiful: Starfighters spin and whirl as they jockey for position, lit by colorful flashes of explosions and laser fire. All the same, at Ryloth, Tucker wishes he were watching from farther away.

ONE OF HONDO OHNAKA'S lieutenants, Turk Falso has never liked taking orders from his pirate boss. When a rich shipment of spice arrives from the Republic, Turk sees a chance to make his own fortune. And he might have succeeded, if not for the interference of a meddling Gungan.

TURK FALSO
BAD LIEUTENANT

Bandanna from days in swoop gang

Florrum's dust storms are hard on the skin

A THIEF'S HONOR

Turk decides to take a chance at a fortune when Hondo sends him to escort the Republic shuttle carrying spice to ransom Count Dooku. On Turk's orders, Barb Mentir shoots the ship down instead, and Turk heads for the crash site on a speeder bike with several other thugs. Today is payday!

Lace-up boots stolen from rich captive

STATISTICS

SPECIES: Weequay

HEIGHT: 1.92 m (6 ft 3 in)

GENDER: Male

ALLEGIANCE: Himself

HOMEWORLD: Sriluur

WEAPONS: LL-30 blaster pistol

TALENTS: Swoop-bike piloting; scheming; drinking grog

KNOWN COMPANIONS: Hondo Ohnaka, Pilf Mukmuk

CAPTAIN TYPHO IS PADMÉ Amidala's head of security. This is a tough job given the hatred for the Naboo Senator among high-ranking Separatist leaders. For dedicated Typho, the question isn't if danger will return—but when.

Eye lost during Battle of Naboo

Cuirass of tough nerf hide

Shinguards worn over work boots

STATISTICS

SPECIES: Human
HEIGHT: 1.85 m (6 ft 1 in)
GENDER: Male
ALLEGIANCE: Naboo
HOMEWORLD: Naboo
WEAPONS: S-5 heavy blaster pistol
TALENTS: Combat; security expert
KNOWN COMPANIONS: Padmé Amidala, Queen Neeyutnee

A WARY EYE

Typho protects not just Padmé, but also the planet Naboo. He knows the leaders of the Trade Federation would love to despoil his homeworld as revenge for their humiliation in the Battle of Naboo years before.

DURING THE SECOND BATTLE of Geonosis, the Republic makes a grim discovery: Geonosian warriors can fight on after their deaths if the remains of their minds are controlled by hive-mind parasites. This means they form an army of undead.

Prongs protect vulnerable neck

Parasite controls nervous system

UNDEAD GEONOSIAN
CATACOMB ZOMBIES

STATISTICS

SPECIES: Geonosian
HEIGHT: 1.7 m (5 ft 7 in)
GENDER: Male
ALLEGIANCE: Separatists
HOMEWORLD: Geonosis
WEAPONS: Claws, numbers
EQUIPMENT: Wings, chitin armor

Torn wings prevent further flight

Foot lost to age or accident

DARK DOOM

Veteran clone troopers have seen many terrible things during the war tearing apart the galaxy. But the bloodiest battle is no preparation for the horror of what they find in the warm dark beneath the Progate Temple: A shambling army of silent, zombie warriors.

STATISTICS

SPECIES: Battle droid
HEIGHT: 3.5 m (11 ft 6 in)
GENDER: No gender programmed
ALLEGIANCE: Separatists
MANUFACTURER: Baktoid/ Haor Chall
WEAPONS: Blaster cannons
EQUIPMENT: Droid brain, sensors, fuel cells

Cognitive module housing

Flight assault laser cannon

Port wing in attack mode

VULTURE DROID
STARFIGHTER SENTINELS

A NUMBERS GAME

An individual droid starfighter is no match for even a rookie clone pilot—the droids' attack patterns are predictable and unimaginative. But rarely does a pilot encounter just one vulture droid: Separatist ships launch them in vast waves, and those attack patterns form a dense, deadly web of laser blasts that even the best pilot can't escape for very long.

WAG TOO
LURMEN HEALER

STATISTICS

SPECIES: Lurmen
HEIGHT: 1.03 m (3 ft 5 in)
GENDER: Male
ALLEGIANCE: Neutral
HOMEWORLD: Maridun
WEAPONS: None
TALENTS: Scouting; agility; healing
KNOWN COMPANIONS: Tee Watt Kaa, Tub

Simple cap made from felt

A HEALER LIVES HERE

Tee Watt Kaa fears that the Jedi and clone troopers will poison the peaceful atmosphere he has worked hard to create on the harsh world of Maridun. But he can't ignore the refugees' pleas that one of their party needs help—and his son Wag Too is a skilled healer.

Sharp ears detect sounds of trouble

Long arms evolved for travel in trees

Tail held out straight for balance

THE FOREMAN OF THE Techno Union, Wat Tambor presides over the occupation of Ryloth. He is used to the high pressure of Skako, and needs his protective suit to survive in other environments. Without it he would burst like a green balloon.

Skin stretched tight over skull

Vocabular processes Skakoan speech

STATISTICS

SPECIES: Skakoan

HEIGHT: 1.61 m (5 ft 3 in)

GENDER: Male

ALLEGIANCE: Separatists

HOMEWORLD: Skako

WEAPONS: None

TALENTS: Engineering; logistics; leadership

KNOWN COMPANIONS: Count Dooku, General Grievous, Nute Gunray

Rich outer tunic over exo-suit

WAT TAMBOR
EMIR OF RYLOTH

STAYING PUT

TA-175 shows Tambor what his droid spies have discovered: Mace Windu is nearing the city of Lessu with clone troopers and Twi'lek guerrillas. But Skakoan refuses to evacuate while Ryloth still has riches he can steal.

ASSIGNED TO RECON DUTIES with Boil, Waxer is searching a Twi'lek city when he finds a little girl named Numa. His good deed of looking after her is repaid when Numa helps the clone troopers pierce the Separatist defenses and win a critical battle.

Head shaved bald for quick grooming

Colors indicate Ghost Company

WAXER
COMPASSIONATE CLONE

STATISTICS

SPECIES: Human

HEIGHT: 1.83 m (6 ft)

GENDER: Male

ALLEGIANCE: Republic

HOMEWORLD: Kamino

WEAPONS: DC-15 blaster pistol

TALENTS: Combat, recon, and military tactics

KNOWN COMPANIONS: Boil, Numa, Commander Cody

"Bucket" taken off to reassure frightened girl

ADVANCE ON NABAT

The approach to Nabat isn't easy: The droid TX-20 has ringed the city with battle droids dug into the former homes of Twi'leks. A quick reconnaissance shows the Republic forces the unhappy truth: It will take a frontal assault to break into the occupied city.

STATISTICS

SPECIES: Kerkoiden
HEIGHT: 1.75 m (5 ft 9 in)
GENDER: Male
ALLEGIANCE: Separatists
HOMEWORLD: Kerkoidia
WEAPONS: Blaster rifle
TALENTS: Military tactics; handling weapons
KNOWN COMPANIONS: Asajj Ventress, General Grievous

Broad head evolved for burrowing in soil

Ceremonial uniform of Kerkoiden cavalier

Fauld in honor of previous victories

WHORM LOATHSOM
SEPARATIST TACTICIAN

BAD MANNERS

Obi-Wan Kenobi seems so civilized that Whorm agrees to discuss his surrender over a cup of tarine tea: There's no reason why enemies on the battlefield must act like savages once the shooting stops. But Kenobi is stalling, and he turns the tables on Whorm. How uncivilized!

CC-3636, WHO HAS earned the nickname "Wolffe," serves Plo Koon as leader of the close-knit squad, the Wolfpack. He is tireless in his efforts against the Seps and takes his cue from his General's ferocity in battle—an attitude shared by the rest of his squad.

Cybernetic eye replaces real one

WOLFFE
ALPHA TROOPER OF THE WOLFPACK

STATISTICS

SPECIES: Human
HEIGHT: 1.83 m (6 ft)
GENDER: Male
ALLEGIANCE: Republic
HOMEWORLD: Kamino
WEAPONS: DC-15 blaster pistol
TALENTS: Combat; military strategy; leadership
KNOWN COMPANIONS: Boost, Sinker, Plo Koon

Helmet bears wolf markings

SIDELINED

Commander Wolffe is serving a duty rotation out of armor when the *Triumphant* is attacked by General Grievous's flagship *Malevolence*. Without armor, Wolffe can only stand by and watch as battle droids hunt the escape pod he's in with Boost, Sinker, and Plo Koon. For a man of action, it's a frustrating situation.

Armor has seen many a fight

BATLIKE HUNTERS WITH six eyes and four wings, xandu haunt the canyons of Iego, looking for prey, which they seize in their talons and carry off to devour or dash against the rocks hundreds of meters below. But beware—even worse things live on Iego's canyon floors.

Broad wings ride the slightest breeze

Keen ears for tracking prey

STATISTICS

SPECIES: Xandu
HEIGHT: 3.62 m (11 ft 11 in)
HOMEWORLD: Iego
ATTACKS: Wing rush, drop prey
ECOLOGY: Xandu hunt for prey in the canyons of Iego and the lightless realm below

XANDU
CANYON HUNTER

Strong jaws finish off wounded prey

Vestigial fingers top leathery wings

Long legs help on quick takeoffs

GOING DOWN!

Anakin and Obi-Wan descend into Iego's canyons in search of reeksa root, a key ingredient in preparing an antidote to the Blue Shadow Virus. It's a quick trip after a xandu spies them and scoops them up for a terrifying ride to the bottom.

LEADER OF THE JEDI Order, Yoda is determined to save the Republic, but is troubled by the Jedi's new job of commanding clones and waging war as Generals in the Republic military. He fears the Order may lose its way even if it proves victorious.

YODA
GRAND MASTER OF THE JEDI

Small lightsaber packs deadly punch

Head has been bald for centuries

Simple, rough robe of worn cloth

STATISTICS

SPECIES: Unknown
HEIGHT: 66 cm (2 ft 2 in)
GENDER: Male
ALLEGIANCE: Jedi Order
HOMEWORLD: Coruscant
WEAPONS: Lightsaber
TALENTS: Force-sensitivity; master of all lightsaber styles; battle meditation; diplomacy; leadership; knowledge of Jedi traditions
KNOWN COMPANIONS: Mace Windu, Obi-Wan Kenobi, Anakin Skywalker, Chancellor Palpatine

STUDENTS AND TEACHER

On Rugosa's ruined coral moon, Yoda accepts Asajj Ventress's wager for the loyalty of Toydaria's King Katuunko. He has only just three clone troopers, while Ventress commands hundreds of battle droids. It's not a fair fight, the Jedi Master thinks—Ventress has no idea how much trouble awaits her.

A HERO OF BATTLES against pirates and slavers, Yularen is amazed by Anakin Skywalker's skill with the Force, but worries about the young Jedi's lack of discipline. A warship cannot be effective if its officers think that it's fine to ignore orders.

Eyebrow arched in skepticism

Badge shows military rank

Gloves are an officer's tradition

STATISTICS

SPECIES: Human
HEIGHT: 1.81 m (5 ft 11 in)
GENDER: Male
ALLEGIANCE: Republic
HOMEWORLD: Anaxes
WEAPONS: DC-17 hand blaster
TALENTS: Master of military tactics; intelligence; expert marksman; respected for years of Naval service
KNOWN COMPANIONS: Anakin Skywalker, Ahsoka Tano, Captain Rex

YULAREN
WITNESS TO HISTORY

ON THE BRIDGE

At the center of a Republic warship's bridge is her captain, who should remain cool and calm even if men are dying around him. Yularen's father taught him that, and the admiral considers it his duty to pass on the lesson to any officer who serves alongside him.

THIS ANCIENT CREATURE IS found, accidentally, beneath the surface of Malastare, taken captive, and brought to Coruscant, where its scales might be used to create tougher armor for clone troopers. When it breaks free of its chains, no one in the vast city is safe.

ZILLO BEAST
DWELLER IN THE DEPTHS

Spiked tail strikes with great force

Jaws can bite through metal

Scales are light but very tough

THE MONSTER OF CORUSCANT

The Zillo Beast isn't obviously intelligent, but Sionver Boll wonders if the creature understands what is happening to it. It certainly seems to know Chancellor Palpatine is its enemy: When the Zillo escapes its prison, it zeroes in on the Senate building in hopes of killing the man who has ordered its torment.

STATISTICS

SPECIES: Hutt
LENGTH: 3.9 m (12 ft 10 in)
GENDER: Male
ALLEGIANCE: Himself
HOMEWORLD: Sleheyron
WEAPONS: None
TALENTS: Running a criminal organization; political dealmaking
KNOWN COMPANIONS: Count Dooku, Cad Bane

JABBA THE HUTT'S UNCLE Ziro controls his own criminal organization based in the Coruscant underworld. The scheming Ziro seeks to topple Jabba by working with Count Dooku to kidnap his nephew's young son, Rotta. By drawing Jabba into a fight with the Republic, Ziro will profit.

ZIRO THE HUTT
HUTT SCHEMER

Feathers from an Ulmatran condor

ZIRO'S UNDOING

Ziro's plan goes awry when he decides that Padmé Amidala is too dangerous to be left alive and must disappear. The crafty Senator gets a message to her protocol droid, who sends the Coruscant Guard to save her and take Ziro into custody.

Ziro loves gaudy rings and bangles

Tattoos inked by Sleheyroni artist

Symbol of Ziro's Black Sun faction

**LONDON, NEW YORK,
MELBOURNE, MUNICH AND DELHI**

SENIOR EDITOR: Elizabeth Dowsett
MANAGING EDITOR: Catherine Saunders
ART DIRECTOR: Lisa Lanzarini
CATEGORY PUBLISHER: Simon Beecroft
PRODUCTION EDITOR: Clare McLean
PRODUCTION CONTROLLER: Nick Seston

Designed for DK by Anne Sharples

At Lucasfilm
EXECUTIVE EDITOR: J. W. Rinzler
KEEPER OF THE HOLOCRON: Leland Chee
IMAGE ARCHIVES: Stacy Cheregotis, Stacey Leong, Tina Mills
ART DIRECTOR: Troy Alders
DIRECTOR OF PUBLISHING: Carol Roeder

First published in the United States in 2010 by DK Publishing
375 Hudson Street, New York, New York 10014

10 11 12 13 14 10 9 8 7 6
009-177925—04/10

A catalog record for this book is available
from the Library of Congress.

ISBN: 978-0-7566-6308-7

Color reproduction by
Media Development and Printing Ltd, UK.
Printed and bound in China by Leo Paper Products.

Dorling Kindersley would like to thank Jo Casey and Shari Last
for their editorial work.

Discover more at
www.dk.com
www.starwars.com